COUNTRY TRADITIONS

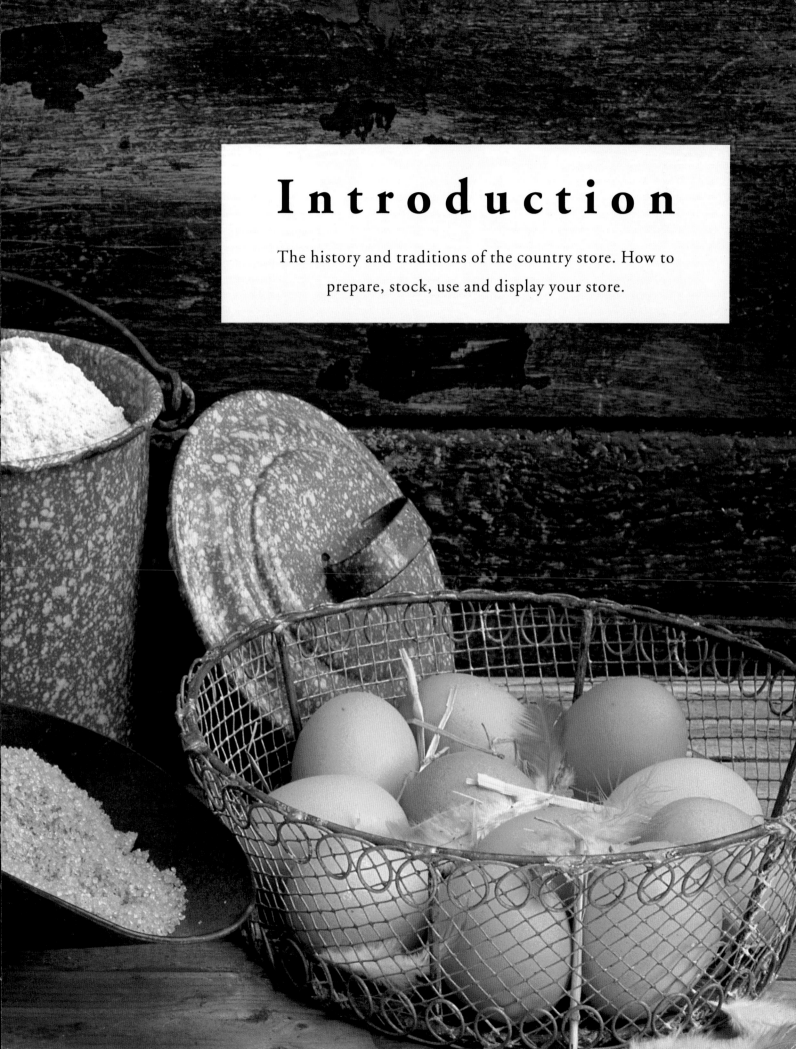

Introduction

The history and traditions of the country store. How to prepare, stock, use and display your store.

A simpler way of life

Our constant search for progress has resulted in a world where, for many of us, the seasons have become largely irrelevant, except as a backdrop for a change of clothing and sporting activities. We can eat fresh cherries from Chile in January, avocados from Israel throughout the year, and, like spoilt children, indulge our every culinary whim regardless of the time of year. The price we pay for this progress is not just the cost of these unseasonal foods, but it is also an alienation from our deepest instincts to sow and reap and store, to mark the change of the seasons in festivals and thanksgiving and to pass on the knowledge of these things to future generations.

There is still a hunger in us for these old ways, and although few of us regret the advent of many of modern life's labour-saving devices and comforts, we are drawn to the simplicity of earlier times when survival was a reward rather than an expectation. Although we no longer need to follow the progress of the seasons to ensure our survival, we can still participate in seasonal activities and will find our lives immeasurably enriched by doing so.

The sowing of seeds, even if it is just a pot of parsley on the windowsill, is the beginning of a relationship with the plants that germinate, the picking of apples from the garden follows the beauty of the spring blossom and the slow growth of the tiny green fruit to their full-flushed maturity when we can enjoy the satisfaction of our own harvest.

I hope very much that *The Country Store* will inspire you to take some time out of our busy and hectic modern life to experience for yourself the pleasure of the seasons: to discover the enjoyment to be had in baking, pickling and preserving; to try the simple natural remedies and fragrant beauty products and potpourris; and to celebrate the progress of the year with seasonal decorations and foods.

Right: *An assortment of invaluable items to collect for your still room: blocks of beeswax, candles, flower waters, essential oils, dried herbs and flowerheads.*

The history of the store cupboard

In the Middle Ages, the monasteries were the repositories of knowledge, and high ranking amongst the monks was the cellarer who had overall responsibility for providing the religious community with all the food and drink that was needed throughout the year. He was an expert in the growing, harvesting and preserving of large quantities of food, and while life in general was short and not very sweet, the religious orders were well nourished and far healthier than the general populace. The cellarer's knowledge of herbs and spices, of salts, vinegars and oils increased as new plants and flavourings were introduced from other lands, and his uses of them, as well as his observations, were meticulously recorded in what were the forebears of our modern recipe books.

In Elizabethan England it became customary for gentlewomen to write down the secrets of their household management in a book to pass on their skills from one generation to the next. As well as recipes, this book would include simple remedies, lotions and potions, potpourris and polishes, many of which we would recognize and even keep in our store cupboard today.

As the ability to read and write spread amongst the population, this tradition was taken up more generally, and for generations families and friends passed on and exchanged family recipes to keep the store cupboard full. It was not until Victorian times, and the advent of tomes such as Mrs Beeton's *Book of Household Management*, that this knowledge passed from the family into the hands of "experts" and began to acquire a mystique which removed it from its common part of our everyday lives.

Above: *In the past, salt was of great social and economic importance and was an extremely valuable commodity.*

Left: *In former times, all but the poorest households would have owned a cow and the dairy was as important as the still room to the countrywoman.*

Right: *Blue and white enamelware is enduringly popular, and is appreciated for its durability, practicality and simple design.*

Traditions, folklore and fact

In the days when good husbandry was an essential skill for every country dweller, the circle of the seasons entailed an endless progression of tasks that had to be completed to ensure the fertility and productivity of the land followed by a fruitful harvest that would see the family through the long winter. Everyone had their tasks: even the smallest of the children would be put to work picking stones, scaring the birds and gathering fruit and vegetables. As the daughters grew up they would learn the skills of the kitchen, the dairy and still room from their mother, and by the time they left to make their own homes, they would be accomplished in all the necessary tasks of everyday life. For everyone, such important festivals as Easter, Harvest Festival, Thanksgiving and Christmas were markers in the year, and these celebrations were rewards for the hard work of daily life as well as religious occasions.

Many folk tales and traditional rhymes were originally devised as a reminder of the seasonal tasks. In Tudor England, for example, the poet and writer Thomas Tusser was particularly free with his advice, instructing farmer and housewife alike in books with edifying titles

Below: *Preparing food for the table was a lengthy task. Vegetables would have to be picked from the garden, scrubbed clean and then peeled before being chopped up for the pot.*

such as *Five Hundred Points of Good Husbandry* and *Housewifely Admonitions*. A typical example of his rhyming recommendations is this little verse on the efficacy of wormwood to prevent the infestation of houses by fleas:

> *While wormwood hath seed, get a bundle or twain,*
> *to save against March, to make flea to refrain:*
> *Where chamber is sweept, and wormwood is strown,*
> *no flea, for his life, dare abide to be known.*

In other words, wormwood should be picked when it has set seed in the late summer or autumn, hung up to dry over winter and then used at the time of spring cleaning in early spring, when it will be most effective against fleas. In an age when books were a luxury, such rhymes made it easier to remember advice and knowledge.

Above: *Making jams and preserves would have been an activity that the whole family joined in, from collecting fruits from the hedgerows around the house or farm to helping mother with the cooking – and eating – of the produce.*

Although superstition and folklore certainly played their part in rural life, country people have always been, by and large, great realists and were far too busy working to spend much time on spells and potions. These were largely the province of doctors and charlatans, whose cures were frequently more dangerous than the illness itself. Country people preferred to rely on simple remedies which every housewife prepared in her still room. Just as we once again appreciate the quality of home-made preserves and provender, so we are also acknowledging that many of the old remedies were based on understanding rather than superstition.

Preparing your store

It is quite possible to make practically everything shown in this book without having to buy any special equipment, but the projects will be easier to do if you have a good range of basic kitchen equipment. The following items are recommended.

• a large, heavy-based pan for preserving and sterilizing
• a good selection of clean glass jars and bottles
• fresh rubber seals for preserving jars
• accurate scales
• measuring jugs
• a selection of mixing bowls
• a *bain-marie* or double boiler – if you are also going to make cosmetics, you will need a second bowl to fit your saucepan, which you should keep purely for this purpose. Also keep a set of the following utensils for cosmetics only:
• metal whisk
• wooden spoon
• set of measuring spoons

BASIC MATERIALS AND INGREDIENTS

If you are fortunate enough to live in the country, you may already have a productive garden and access to fruitful hedgerows and woodlands to provide many of the basic materials from which you can begin to fill your country store, but for those of us less blessed, there is still the pleasure of making, even if we do not do the growing and the gathering ourselves. The best farm shops are a good source of freshly picked fruit and vegetables, as are the farms where you can pick your own produce. Even city dwellers will find many bargains at their local market, especially at the end of the day when a whole box can be bought at a knock-down price. An elderly neighbour whose garden is becoming neglected may welcome your planting a vegetable patch and sharing the produce with them. And in a fruitful year, a friend with an apple tree will consider you are doing them a favour if you ask for some fruit.

Everyone should grow some herbs. They give our food savour, stimulate the appetite, are health-giving and a fragrant addition to the home. Herbs are widely used in the projects in this book, and whatever the scale of your herb garden, whether a windowsill or a formal garden, you will be able to make use of everything you grow.

Left: *Use a wire basket for picking produce; excess soil can drop through the base and good air circulation keeps the vegetables in prime condition for several days.*

Below: *Fresh ingredients, whether home-grown or bought, are the starting point and the inspiration for everything you will make for your store cupboard.*

Above: There is an intrinsic beauty to old, well-used kitchen utensils and equipment, and provided they do the job and can be properly cleaned, there is no need to replace them.

Right: Cox's Orange Pippin apples may not have the glossy perfection of some other varieties, but their flavour is unsurpassed.

Whether you are collecting ingredients for cooking, for natural remedies, for fragrance or celebration, it is vitally important that they are always of the highest possible quality. For example, for bottling, fully ripe but firm fruit will give the best flavour. Herbs are at their most potent just before they flower. Vegetables should be used as soon as possible after they have been picked or bought. Essential oils should always be purchased from a reputable supplier, and dried flowers should be from the most recent harvest. In other words, quite simply, if your intention is to make a quality product, you must use only quality ingredients.

Growing and gathering for your store

One of the great advantages of growing your own produce is that you know precisely what has been used on the plants: no over-enthusiastic applications of fertilizers or other chemicals. Ideally, just the sweat of your brow and lots of compost. If possible grow your vegetables, fruit and herbs organically because they will be better for you and organic cultivation is also better for the health of the soil. If you do need to control pests, try to use natural predators wherever possible. They are increasingly available and as effective as chemical sprays when used correctly.

BUYING FOR YOUR STORE

Organically grown foods are also available from specialist food stores and some supermarkets. While they do not always have the glossy perfection of their chemically stimulated relatives, their flavour is generally excellent. Remember that what you wish to preserve in your country store is flavour and fragrance, so it is important to choose varieties that have these attributes; a visually perfect and glowing red apple that has the texture of cotton wool will not taste any better once it has been bottled.

GATHERING FOR YOUR STORE

Fortunately, it is now easier to collect fruits, berries and nuts from the hedgerows as the days when farmers and highway maintenance teams sprayed our roadsides with weedkillers are mostly past. There is a welcome return of a profusion of wild flowers that make verges and field margins so lovely in the spring and summer months and a corresponding burgeoning of hedgerows with abundant elderflowers, blackberries, sloes, hips and haws. When gathering from the wild, always do so respectfully. Always make sure that you leave plenty for the wildlife, as the hedgerow is an important food source for them, and also something for others who would like to share in nature's bounty. Never pick an endangered species. It is your responsibility to find out which plants are protected in your area and it is important that you do so; your local council or library will be able to help you.

Anyone who has gathered blackberries, sloes or wild strawberries will tell you that it takes a surprisingly long time to collect a usable quantity, and it always seems that the best and most plenteous fruit is just out of reach. So make gathering a group activity, preferably with people of varying heights and including someone with a hooked stick to reach those elusive branches. What can be a chore for an individual can be fun for the whole family who will also benefit from the fresh air and exercise.

Right: *Home-grown peas have an unrivalled flavour and shelling them while sitting in the sunshine is a restful occupation.*

Above: *Sow small quantities of seeds frequently in order to provide a succession of produce throughout the season.*

Above: *Beetroot thinnings provide delicious baby beets and the leaves can be cooked just like spinach.*

Right: *Gather your herbs in the morning when they are at their most aromatic and pick regularly.*

HARVESTING FOR YOUR STORE

This is the time when your efforts are rewarded, when those carefully nurtured fruits, vegetables, blossoms and herbs are gathered in ready to be used to fill your store. Choose your harvest time carefully; a dry sunny day with a light breeze is ideal – for you and the produce. Flowers and herbs should be gathered only after the dew has dried but before midday. You must pick fruit carefully to avoid bruising or damaging them in any way. Young vegetables should be gathered in small batches for immediate use and mature root vegetables lifted before the first frosts.

Using and displaying your store cupboard

There is a temptation to treat the contents of the store cupboard rather like works of art, treasures to be displayed and admired but never touched, but this is to miss out on the best bit of all – the consumption. Once you have tasted and enjoyed the fruits of your labours, it becomes easier to accept that your country store is an ever-changing Aladdin's cave of treats and temptations rather than an end in itself.

If considerations of space, time and money permit it, then a cool, dark larder or cellar is the perfect place to keep jams, pickles and preserves, but failing that, set aside a cupboard in your kitchen for storing home-made produce. Warm, light rooms are not ideal for the storage of preserves or for drying flowers and herbs, but if you dry some flowers and herbs especially for display and have a pretty shelf where you can show off your preserves for a short period before use, then you can keep the majority of your produce in good condition while not missing out on the compliments.

Above: *Miniature galvanized buckets can be used as attractive containers for a collection of medicinal herbs and flowers.*

Left: *Turn your fresh herbs into an attractive feature in a room by storing them in pretty glass containers.*

Right: *Autumn leaves and bows made out of raffia or coarse string can give your jars of preserves an attractive rustic finish.*

Decorating and presenting

The finishing touches can turn an everyday item into something special. A simple pot of jam, for instance, becomes a special gift when it is presented in a pretty jar with the lid covered by a beautiful autumn leaf tied on with raffia. And a bottle of aromatic chilli oil does not need a written label to identify its flavourings when its neck is decorated with a bunch of chillis.

Colourful sweetmeats are all the more tempting for being individually packaged in cellophane and tied with a raffia bow, or nestling inside a decorative wooden box.

Celebration wines and ratafias become sublime when bottled in decorative glass bottles and adorned with gilded leaves and corks.

Above: *A decorative touch turns this lemon- and lime-flavoured vinegar into a perfect gift.*

Above: *Natural materials make inexpensive packaging.*

Left: *A dried orange slice tied around a jar of marmalade is an unusual but eloquent label.*

Right: *The autumnal colours of the potpourri are echoed in the matt-brown ribbon and the sisal string used to decorate the cellophane bag.*

The Pantry

An irresistible collection of preserves and pickles, flavoured oils and vinegars, baked goods and sweet gifts.

Fruit and vegetables

Whether the fruit and vegetables you use are from your own garden or from elsewhere, produce that is destined for preserving should always be of the best possible quality. When growing your own produce, choose the varieties whose good flavour is particularly mentioned. It is amazing how many modern varieties that are grown for disease resistance and reliability seem to have totally sacrificed flavour in the search for the standardization of colour and size. Therefore, if you are buying fruit and vegetables, it is always a good idea to taste them before you start preserving, just to make sure that they have a flavour that is worth keeping. Less than perfect fruit such as windfalls can be used to make jellies, but because they deteriorate quickly, you should be ready for action as soon as you have collected them.

Wherever possible, store your fruit and vegetables in a dark, cool but frost-free place with good ventilation. They will keep extremely well in these conditions, especially if they are prepared for storage beforehand. Mature root vegetables such as carrots, parsnips and beetroots will keep for months when stored in boxes of sand (it must be horticultural, not builder's, sand). Apples and pears can be kept on slatted wooden shelves, if they are not touching, or you can individually wrap them in paper and store them in boxes. They should last through the winter, especially if the varieties stored are good keepers such as Russet apples and Conference pears.

You must never store fruit near potatoes because it will become tainted. It is important to check your stored fruit and vegetables regularly, using the fruit as it ripens and removing any that shows signs of rot or this will spread through the good fruit.

Below: *The flavour of tomatoes is improved by storing them at room temperature rather than in a refrigerator. Ideally, tomatoes should not be picked until they are fully ripe, but even an under-ripe fruit will improve if you store it in this way.*

Above: *In autumn, prepare
unblemished apples for storage
during the winter. Each fruit
should be wrapped in newspaper and stored on a wooden
tray or in a cardboard box.
Alternatively, store them
unwrapped and not touching
on slatted, wooden shelves.*

Right: *The traditional way of
storing mature root vegetables
is to arrange them in layers in
silver sand. Then cover them
completely and store in a cool,
dark place and they will keep
for months, retaining a good
flavour and texture.*

Herbs and flowers

If you have enough space in your garden, devoting a corner to the growing of herbs and flowers for drying will save you a great deal of money.

Herbs vary enormously in their aromatic strength and it is worth the time and expense to find a reputable herb grower who can sell you recommended named varieties of the herbs. If you do not have space to grow all the herbs you will need, there are companies which sell good-quality fresh and dried herbs by mail order far more cheaply than you can buy them at a supermarket. It is also worthwhile visiting shops which cater for Indian and South-East Asian communities as a source of high-quality herbs and spices.

Herbs should be harvested before they have flowered, on a dry morning when the volatile oils will be at their most concentrated. From noon onwards the oils start to evaporate into the surrounding air and flavour and fragrance are diminished.

Although herbs look very decorative when hung in open bunches from an old-fashioned clothes-airer, this is not the best way to dry them. Rather, the bunches of herbs should be rolled up in cones of brown paper, which will protect them from the light, then hung up to dry. Once they are fully dry (usually about two weeks), they should be taken down, stripped from their stems and stored in coloured glass bottles away from the light. This will ensure that when you come to use the herbs for cooking or fragrance, they will still be intensely aromatic.

When growing flowers for drying, it is worth concentrating on the varieties that are difficult to come by or expensive, such as paeonies and roses. Unless you have limitless space, there is little point in growing huge quantities of statice and helichrysum which can be bought easily and inexpensively.

When picking flowers for drying, they should be in full bloom but not full blown or they will drop their petals. They are also best gathered in the morning of a dry day. Hang them upside down in bunches in a warm, preferably not too light position and leave them there until they are dry to the touch. Paeonies need to be dry right

Left: *A simple but very effective method of preserving your fresh herbs is to place them in a jar with a tight-fitting lid that contains sea salt. The herbs will then remain just as fresh and full of flavour as the day they were picked, and they will also give a delicious and distinctive flavour to the salt.*

Above: *Fresh herbs should be picked early in the day to capture the full intensity of their flavour. Keep them cool indoors until you are ready to use them, and replace them as soon as they start to look rather limp and bedraggled.*

Left: *The best way to dry fresh flowers is to tie them loosely in small bundles and hang them upside-down in a well-ventilated room. Keep them out of direct sunlight to retain their vibrant colours.*

into the centre of the flower and, to achieve this, it is advisable to place them in a low oven for about four hours after they have air-dried. Once you are confident that your flowers are fully dry, pack them into boxes and store in a dry place until you wish to use them. It is important to store dried flowers in boxes in order to keep them free of dust and preserve their colour.

When buying dried flowers, it is best to purchase them from the grower, as these will have been stored in the best possible conditions and will not have been handled many times which often happens to dried flowers before they reach your local shop. Bargain dried flowers are nearly always old stock from the harvest before last and are not worth buying as they are brittle and faded.

Preserving produce

Preserving and drying are time-honoured methods for prolonging the life of fruit, vegetables, herbs and sometimes flowers.

PRESERVING

Food can be preserved by being bottled in a variety of natural preservatives. Vegetables and herbs may be preserved by being packed in salt or immersed in brine. They can also be kept in oil, or used in small amounts to flavour oil. Vegetables, fruit and herbs can be pickled in or used to flavour vinegar and lemon juice. Even sugar and honey can be used for preserving fruit, herbs and flowers or can be flavoured by them. Fruit, herbs and flowers can also be preserved in alcohol or turned into wines and liqueurs.

DRYING

Vegetables, herbs, fruit and flowers can all be preserved by being air-dried or placed in an oven set at a low temperature.

STERILIZING JARS IN WATER

1 *Line the base of the sterilizing pan with either a folded cloth or a wooden trivet.*

2 *Place the bottles in the pan and fold cloths around each one to prevent them touching.*

3 *Fill the pan with cold water so that the bottles are covered by at least 2.5cm/1in of water.*

4 *Once the sterilizing is complete and the bottles have cooled, check the seals by loosening the clips and making sure that they stay intact.*

STERILIZING

To ensure that harmful bacteria are eliminated from fruit and vegetables bottled in brine, syrup or their own juices, it is necessary to sterilize the bottles in a water bath or in the oven. To sterilize in water, follow the step instructions on the facing page. Alternatively, rest the lids on the bottles but do not seal. Stand them on a baking sheet lined with newspaper and place in a very low oven,

Above: *Whether dried, bottled in syrup or preserved in oil, there is a surprising but striking beauty to many home-made preserves.*

120°C/250°F/Gas ½. Remove and seal immediately. As the bottles cool, a vacuum forms inside to complete the seal. Always use clean, undamaged bottles with fresh seals, and test every seal by turning it upside down. Bottles with failed seals should be used immediately.

29

Choosing and preparing containers

Glass jars and bottles have been used for the majority of projects in this chapter. Glass is durable, versatile and decorative. Its great advantage over aluminium, earthenware, terracotta, tin and porcelain is that it reveals and enhances its contents. Modern recycled glass has many of the qualities of antique glass such as flaws and colourings, and is inexpensive. Old-fashioned sweet jars, preserving jars and jam pots can still be bought in junk shops and, providing that they can be properly cleaned, used to great effect. However, they must not be used for any bottling that requires sterilizing.

STERILIZING JARS

To sterilize jars in a dishwasher, use the hottest wash but without any detergent. However, if you do not own a dishwasher, you can sterilize in the following way. First, wash the jars in hot, soapy water and rinse thoroughly. Stand them the right way up on a wooden board (making sure that they are not touching) and place the board in a cold oven. Turn the oven to very low (110°C/225°F/Gas ¼) and leave the jars for 30 minutes. If they are not to be used immediately, cover with a clean cloth.

Above: *Old-fashioned glass bottles are full of character and very attractive. They may be used for projects where containers should be clean but not necessarily sterile.*

Above: *There is a variety of bottles and jars that are designed especially for preserving, and provided they are not damaged in any way, they can be reused. However, you should always use fresh seals.*

19.6.95

SEALS

The type and effectiveness of the seal required depend on the process used. Providing jam jars are thoroughly washed and dried before use, a circle of greaseproof paper and a paper cover are sufficient to keep the contents in good condition. Wines and liqueurs keep well in bottles sealed with new corks. Vinegars and oils can be sealed with either corks or screw tops, but bottled fruit and vegetables must be sealed with new rubber seals.

Ideally, all your preserves should be labelled with a description of the contents and the date they were made. Self-adhesive labels may

Above: *With glass containers a descriptive label is not always necessary, but it is a good idea to record the date the preserve was made so that you use the contents of your store cupboard in rotation.*

be attached to the surface of the bottle or jar or, alternatively, card, wooden or metal labels may be tied round the neck. Bear in mind that if you intend to store your preserves in a cellar or larder where conditions may be slightly damp and paper labels can fall off or quickly deteriorate, it would be advisable to use something more durable such as metal or wooden labels.

Flavoured oils

A selection of flavoured oils will bring the taste of high summer to your cooking all year round. All flavoured oils are best used within three months.

GARLIC OIL

Use this delicious oil in dressings and to brush on fish, meat and vegetables. In addition it saves the fiddly task of cleaning the garlic press every time you flavour with garlic! Do not throw away the poached garlic cloves which are removed from the oil before bottling: they are ambrosial when spread on fresh French bread or used as a relish on meat, fish or vegetables. Either use immediately or pack them into a glass jar, cover with oil and store in a refrigerator to use within ten days.

Makes 750ml/1¼ pints/3 cups
25 large plump garlic cloves
900ml/1½ pints/3¾ cups cold-pressed virgin
*   olive oil*

Above: *Flavoured oils in glass bottles are good to look at as well as useful ingredients.*

1 *Peel the garlic cloves.*

2 *Heat the oil to a gentle simmer in a small pan, then add the garlic cloves and poach them for approximately 25 minutes, until tender and translucent. Leave in the saucepan until cool.*

3 *Strain the garlic cloves from the oil, reserving them for another use. Pour the oil into a clean bottle, seal with a screw top or cork and use within ten days.*

CHILLI OIL

In the south of France, pizzas are enlivened by drizzling chilli oil over them. You can also use this oil for stir-frying vegetables or grilling. For a more robust flavour, add garlic, thyme and peppercorns to this oil.

Makes 500ml/17fl oz/2¼ cups
500ml/17fl oz/2¼ cups virgin olive oil
1 small fresh green chilli
5 small fresh red chillis

Fill a clean, dry bottle with the olive oil. Slice the green chilli crossways into thin rings and add them with the whole red chillis to the oil.

Cork tightly with a new cork and leave to infuse for 10–14 days. Shake the bottle occasionally during this time.

SAFFRON OIL

Saffron has never been surpassed as a flavouring. By weight it is certainly amongst the most expensive of spices but a little saffron goes a long way, especially when you use it to infuse an oil with its delicate flavour and then brush the oil on to grilled fish.

Makes 250ml/8fl oz/1 cup
large pinch saffron strands
250ml/8fl oz/1 cup light olive oil or pure
*   sunflower oil*

Put the saffron strands in a clean dry bottle. Fill the bottle with oil and seal with a cork. Leave to infuse for two weeks, gently shaking the bottle daily, before using.

TERIYAKI MARINADE

This Japanese marinade is wonderful for barbecued and grilled meats. Marinate the meat for at least an hour before cooking.

Makes 375ml/13 fl oz/1½ cups

150ml/¼ pint/⅔ cup olive oil
150ml/¼ pint/⅔ cup soy sauce
2 tbsp grated fresh ginger
2 garlic cloves, crushed
1 tbsp grated orange rind
60ml/4 tbsp dry sherry

Above: *Flavoured oils are a good way of carrying the taste of the summer through into your winter cooking, as the freshness of the herbs and spices is captured in the oil.*

Place all of the ingredients into a wide-necked bottle or jar. Seal the container securely and then shake it vigorously until all the ingredients are thoroughly mixed. Leave the marinade overnight before using. It is best to store it in a cool place, out of direct sunlight.

WARNING: there is some evidence that oils containing fresh herbs and spices can grow harmful moulds, especially once the bottle has been opened and the contents are not fully covered by the oil. To protect against this, it is recommended that the herbs and spices are removed once their flavour has passed into the oil.

Flavoured vinegars

Fruit-flavoured vinegars give a delicious depth to salad dressings and, if used sparingly, will enhance the flavour of fruit such as strawberries and nectarines that are not quite ripe. All flavoured vinegars are best used within three months.

RASPBERRY VINEGAR

Makes 750ml/1¼ pints/3 cups, strained vinegar
600ml/1 pint/2½ cups red wine vinegar
1 tbsp pickling spice
450g/1lb raspberries, fresh or frozen
2 sprigs fresh lemon thyme

Above: *Raspberry vinegar.*

1 *Pour the vinegar into a saucepan, add the spice and heat gently for five minutes.*

2 *Pour the hot vinegar mixture over the raspberries in a bowl and then add the lemon thyme. Cover and leave the mixture to infuse for two days in a cool, dark place, stirring occasionally.*

3 *Remove the thyme and raspberries and strain the liquid. Pour the flavoured vinegar into a clean, dry bottle and seal with a cork.*

LEMON AND LIME VINEGAR

Citrus-flavoured vinegars are wonderful for piquant sauces such as hollandaise.

Makes 600ml/1 pint/2½ cups
600ml/1 pint/2½ cups white wine vinegar
rind of 1 lime (preferably unwaxed)
rind of 1 lemon (preferably unwaxed)

Bring the vinegar to the boil in a saucepan, then pour it over the lime and lemon rind in a bowl. Cover and leave to infuse for three days. Strain and pour it into a clean, dry bottle, adding fresh rind for colour.

ROSEMARY VINEGAR

Herb vinegars are excellent for adding flavour to dressings and sauces.

Makes 600ml/1 pint/2½ cups
600ml/1 pint/2½ cups white wine or cider vinegar
90ml/6 tbsp chopped fresh rosemary plus some whole sprigs

Bring the vinegar to the boil in a saucepan, then pour it over the rosemary in a bowl. Cover and leave to infuse for three days. Strain and pour it into a clean, dry bottle, adding a sprig of rosemary for decoration.

TARRAGON VINEGAR

Make it in exactly the same way as rosemary vinegar, but with tarragon.

Right: *Delicious flavoured vinegars are quick and easy to make.*

Pickles and chutneys

No country store would be complete without a good supply of pickles and chutneys. They are easy to make and the perfect way to deal with a glut of fruit or vegetables. They add a delicious tang to bread and cheese or cold meats, and are always welcome as presents.

KASHMIR CHUTNEY

In the true tradition of the country store, this is a typical family recipe passed down through the generations. It is wonderful with grilled sausages.

Makes approx. 2.75kg/6lb

1kg/2¼lb green apples
15g/½oz garlic cloves
1 litre/1¾ pints/4 cups malt vinegar
450g/1lb dates
115g/4oz preserved ginger
450g/1lb seeded raisins
450g/1lb brown sugar
½ tsp cayenne pepper
25g/1oz salt

Above: *Kashmir chutney.*

1 *Quarter the apples, remove the cores and chop coarsely.*

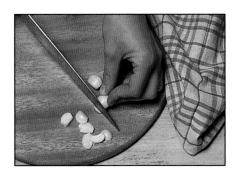

2 *Peel and chop the garlic.*

3 *Place the apple and garlic in a saucepan with enough vinegar to cover and boil until soft. Chop the dates and ginger and add them to the cooked apple and garlic together with all the other ingredients. Boil gently for 45 minutes. Spoon the mixture into sterilized jars and seal immediately.*

GREEN TOMATO CHUTNEY

Unripened tomatoes are a culinary success rather than a horticultural failure when transformed into a delicious chutney.

Makes approx. 2.5kg/5¾lb

1kg/2¼lb green tomatoes
450g/1lb apples
2 medium-size onions
1 litre/1¾ pints/4 cups malt vinegar
425g/15oz brown sugar
250g/9oz sultanas
1½ tsp mustard powder
1 tsp ground cinnamon
¼ tsp ground cloves
¼ tsp cayenne pepper

Quarter the tomatoes and place them in a large preserving pan. Quarter, core and chop the unpeeled apples and add them to the tomatoes. Chop the onions and add them to the tomatoes with all the other ingredients and heat gently, stirring until all the sugar has dissolved. Bring to the boil and simmer uncovered, stirring occasionally, for one and a half hours until the chutney has thickened. Pour the chutney into warm, sterilized jars which should then be sealed immediately.

WINDFALL PEAR CHUTNEY

The seemingly unusable bullet-hard pears that litter the ground beneath old pear trees after high winds respond wonderfully to cooking and can be used to make this tasty chutney.

and add to the pan with the sugar, raspberry vinegar, garlic and salt.

Bring the tomato mixture to the boil over a high heat, stirring occasionally. Reduce the heat and simmer for about one and a half to two hours, stirring regularly, until reduced by half. Purée the mixture in a blender or food mill, then return to the pan and bring to the boil and simmer for 15 minutes.

Bottle in clean, sterilized jars and store in the refrigerator. Use within two weeks.

Above: *Each of these sauces and preserves is a powerful reduction of the main ingredients.*

Alternatively, you can sterilize the ketchup in a water bath or oven (see pages 28 and 29) to keep through the winter.

Flavoured salts and peppers

Flavoured salts and peppers used to be very popular, but they are rarely blended at home these days, as we tend to rely on spice companies to do it for us. This is a pity as they are easy to make, and, when freshly made, have far more flavour than anything that you can buy ready-mixed.

CAYENNE SALT

This adaptation of an old Indian recipe produces flakes of dramatically coloured and wonderfully flavoured salt to use wherever you would use cayenne pepper. Remember, however, not to add any additional salt.

Makes 80g/3oz
2 tbsp sea salt
50g/2oz powdered cayenne pepper
120ml/4fl oz/½ cup white wine

Crush the salt with the cayenne pepper using a mortar and pestle. Add the wine and 250ml/8fl oz/1 cup water to the powdered spices and pour into a bottle. Cork, shake well and stand in a warm place for a week, shaking the mixture from time to

Above: *Sea salt and quails' eggs.*

time. Pour the contents of the bottle into a wide, shallow dish and place in a low oven or a warm place, such as an airing cupboard, until all the liquid has evaporated. Scrape the crystals off the base of the dish and leave to stand overnight to allow any residual moisture to evaporate. Store in a sealed glass jar away from strong light. You could also try making chilli or turmeric salt.

LEMON PEPPER

Dried lemon rind mixed with freshly ground black pepper is a really interesting combination. Try using it on chargrilled fish or in salad dressings.

Makes 125g/4oz
115g/4oz freshly ground coarse black pepper
grated rind of two lemons, dried

Mix the two ingredients and store in a sealed glass jar. This is best used within one month, before the flavours begin to fade.

CELERY SALT

Celery salt is the perfect accompaniment to hard-boiled eggs, especially quails' eggs, which are delicious served as a pre-dinner appetizer with drinks. To make the salt, mix equal amounts of celery seed and sea salt, and leave both whole if you prefer to have a coarser texture, or grind them to a powder using a mortar and pestle.

MIXED PEPPERCORNS

Black, green, white and pink peppercorns each have their own quite distinctive flavour. Mix them in equal proportions and grind them in the normal way just before use for an exotic flavouring. These will keep up to one year if left whole.

Right: *A nest of quails' eggs on a leaf plate, surrounded by flavoured salts and peppers.*

Above: *Cayenne salt crystals.*

Herb and spice mixes

Mixed herbs and spices are readily available in the shops, and we tend to accept that these particular combinations of flavours are the ones to use, but there is no reason why you should not experiment with blending herbs and spices to your own taste. A mortar and pestle are traditionally used to blend the herbs, but using an electric coffee grinder is an easy way to achieve very good results.

LEMON MIX

This combination of lemon flavours makes a wonderful dry marinade for chicken, to be rubbed on to the skin about one hour before roasting or barbecuing.

Makes approx. 50g/2 oz

2 lemons
2 tbsp lemon thyme, chopped
1 tbsp lemon verbena, chopped
1 tbsp lemon grass, chopped

Above: *Lemon mix.*

1 *Peel the lemons into strips and air dry the rind and herbs on a rack for one to two days.*

2 *When thoroughly dry, powder the lemon rind using a mortar and pestle. Add the other flavourings, then crush and blend them together to the desired texture.*

3 *Pack the powdered herbs into fabric bags.*

QUATRE EPICES

This blend of four spices is traditionally used in France for flavouring sausages, pâtés and terrines.

7 parts freshly ground black pepper
1 part freshly grated nutmeg
1 part ground cinnamon
1 part ground cloves

Blend the spices together and pack them into a glass jar. Seal and store away from the light. Use within six months.

MIXED SWEET SPICES

The ready-packaged mixed sweet spices that are available are extremely bland compared with a batch that has been freshly ground and blended. Make it in relatively small quantities and, as with the *quatre epices*, store it in sealed containers away from the light and use within six months. It is a good idea to label the spices with the date they were made so that you know when it is time to throw them out and make a fresh batch.

2 parts dried root ginger
1 part white peppercorns or allspice berries
1 part cloves
1 part nutmeg
1 part cinnamon stick

Grind the whole spices and then blend them together.

Right: *Keep your herbs and spices whole and prepare them only when you need them.*

Flavoured mustards

Making your own mustards is surprisingly easy, and just as with other freshly ground spices, the flavour is far more intense and aromatic than the ready-made versions.

TARRAGON AND CHAMPAGNE MUSTARD

This delicately flavoured mustard is very good with cold seafood or chicken.

Makes approx. 250g/9oz

2 tbsp mustard seed
75ml/5 tbsp champagne vinegar
115g/4oz dry mustard powder
115g/4oz brown sugar
½ tsp salt
50ml/3½ tbsp virgin olive oil
4 tbsp chopped fresh tarragon

Soak the mustard seeds overnight in the vinegar. Pour the mixture into the bowl of a blender, add the mustard powder, sugar and salt and blend until smooth. Slowly add the oil while continuing to blend. Stir in the tarragon. Pour the mustard into sterilized jars, seal and store in a cool place.

HONEY MUSTARD

Honey mustard is richly flavoured and is delicious in sauces and salad dressings.

Makes approx. 500g/1lb 2oz

225g/8oz mustard seeds
1 tbsp ground cinnamon
½ tsp ground ginger
300ml/½ pint/1¼ cups white wine vinegar
90ml/6 tbsp dark runny honey

Mix the mustard seeds with the spices, pour on the vinegar and then leave to soak overnight. Place the mixture in a mortar and pound until you have made a paste, all the while gradually adding the honey. The finished mustard should resemble a stiff paste, so add extra vinegar if necessary. Store the mustard in sterilized jars in the refrigerator. Use within four weeks.

HORSERADISH MUSTARD

Horseradish mustard is a tangy relish that is an excellent accompaniment to cold meats, smoked fish or cheese.

Makes approx. 400g/14oz

25g/1oz mustard seeds
115g/4oz dry mustard powder
115g/4oz sugar
120ml/4fl oz/½ cup white wine or cider vinegar
50ml/2fl oz olive oil
1 tsp lemon juice
2 tbsp horseradish sauce (see page 42)

Place the mustard seeds into a bowl and then pour 250ml/8fl oz/1 cup of boiling water over them and leave for one hour. Drain and place in the bowl of a blender with the remaining ingredients. Blend the mixture into a smooth paste and then spoon it into sterilized jars. Store in the refrigerator and use within three months.

Right: *From left: Honey mustard, Horseradish mustard and Tarragon and champagne mustard.*

Jams, jellies and honeys

Home-made jams, jellies and honeys are the perfect way to deal with a glut of fruit and have an intensity of flavour rare in commercial varieties. Some preserving sugars have added pectin, which means that the jellies and jams need to be boiled for only a few minutes to reach setting point. This simplifies the process, gives consistent results and means that it is quite possible to make a pot or two of jam in under half an hour.

An easy way to test for the setting point is to spoon a little of the mixture on to a chilled saucer. If setting point has been reached, a skin will quickly form on the jelly or jam, which will wrinkle when pushed with the finger. Most jams will benefit if left to stand for 15 minutes before being ladled into jars. This ensures that the pieces of fruit are evenly distributed rather than floating on the top. Some of the following recipes require the use of lemon rind, and preferably unwaxed lemon rind. Provided jams and jellies are properly sealed, they will keep for at least a year in the store cupboard.

CRAB APPLE JELLY

Crab apple trees are so pretty with their abundant flowers and glowing red fruit, and though their role in the garden is mainly decorative, this jelly is a delicious way to make use of the fruit. Serve it with game or use it to glaze an apple tart.

Makes approx. 1kg/2¼lb from each 600ml/1 pint/2½ cups liquid
1kg/2¼lb crab apples
3 cloves
preserving sugar

1 *Wash the apples and halve them, but do not peel or core.*

2 *Place the apples and cloves in a large saucepan and cover with water. Bring to the boil, lower the heat and simmer until soft.*

3 *Strain through muslin or a jelly bag. Warm sugar in a bowl in a low oven (120°C/250°F/Gas ½) for 15 minutes. Measure the juice and add 450g/1lb of sugar for each 600ml/1 pint/2½ cups of juice. Heat gently, stirring until the sugar dissolves, then boil rapidly until setting point is reached. Pour into warmed, sterilized jars and seal.*

ROSEHIP AND APPLE JELLY

This recipe uses windfall apples and rosehips gathered from the hedgerows. The resultant jelly is extremely rich in vitamin C as well as full of flavour. It is excellent with scones or crumpets.

Makes approx. 1kg/2¼lb from each 600ml/1 pint/2½ cups liquid
1kg/2¼lb windfall apples, peeled, trimmed and quartered
450g/1lb firm, ripe rosehips
preserving sugar

Place the quartered apples in a preserving pan with just enough water to cover them, plus 300ml/½ pint/1¼ cups of extra water for the rosehips. Bring to the boil and cook the apples until they are a pulp. Meanwhile, chop the rosehips coarsely in a food processor. Add the rosehips to the cooked apples and leave to simmer for ten minutes, then remove from the heat and allow to stand for a further ten minutes. Leave the mixture to strain overnight through a thick jelly bag.

Measure the juice and allow 400g/14oz sugar for each 600ml/1 pint/2½ cups of liquid. Warm the sugar in the oven. Bring the juice to the boil and stir in the warmed sugar. Stir the mixture until the sugar has completely dissolved, then leave to boil until the setting point is reached. Finally, pour the jelly into warmed, sterilized jars and seal securely.

Right: *A winter sun illuminates the colours of the fruit jellies in a glowing richness.*

RHUBARB AND MINT JELLY

This jelly is an unusual alternative to the usual redcurrant or mint jellies that are traditionally served with lamb.

Makes approx. 1kg/2¼lb from each 600ml/1 pint/2½ cups liquid

1kg/2¼lb young rhubarb
preserving sugar
large bunch fresh mint
2 tbsp finely chopped fresh mint

Cut the rhubarb into pieces, place in a preserving pan, just cover with water and stew until soft. Strain through a jelly bag, measure the juice and allow 450g/1lb of sugar for each 600ml/1 pint/2½ cups of juice. Warm the sugar in the oven. Pour the juice into a preserving pan, add the bunch of mint and the warmed sugar then bring to the boil, stirring until the sugar has dissolved. Boil to setting point, remove the mint bunch and stir in the chopped mint. Bottle in warm, sterilized jars and seal.

DAMSON JAM

There used to be many damson trees growing wild in the hedgerows. Today they are much scarcer, but if you are fortunate enough to have a supply of damsons, this deeply coloured and richly flavoured jam would grace any tea table.

Makes approx. 2kg/4¾lb

1kg/2¼lb damsons
1kg/2¼lb preserving sugar

Place the damsons in a preserving pan, pour in 1.4 litres/2¼ pints/6 cups water and bring to the boil. Reduce the heat and gently simmer until the damsons are soft. Meanwhile, warm the sugar in the oven. Stir in the warmed sugar and bring to the

Above: *Dried apricot jam.*

boil again, skimming off the stones as they rise to the surface (most can be removed this way). Boil to setting point, then leave to stand for ten minutes. Pour the jam into warm, sterilized jars and seal.

DRIED APRICOT JAM

This is a jam which can be made at any time of year, so when reserves in the store cupboard start to look low in late winter, make up a batch of apricot jam and dream of summer months to come.

Makes approx. 2kg/4¾lb

675g/1½lb dried apricots
900ml/1½ pints/3¾ cups apple juice made with concentrate
juice and rind of 2 unwaxed lemons
675g/1½lb preserving sugar
50g/2oz blanched almonds, coarsely chopped

Soak the apricots overnight in the apple juice. Pour the soaked apricots and juice into a preserving pan and add the lemon juice and rind. Bring the mixture to the boil, lower the heat, then leave to simmer for 15-20 minutes, until the apricots are

soft. Meanwhile warm the sugar in the oven. Add the warmed sugar to the apricots and bring to the boil once more, stirring until the sugar has completely dissolved. Boil until setting point is reached. Stir in the chopped almonds and leave to stand for 15 minutes before bottling in warm, sterilized jars and sealing.

ORANGE MARMALADE

Marmalades have been made since the fifteenth century, but the early ones were very different to those eaten today. Then they were fruit pastes or "leathers" while nowadays they are jams made using the peel of citrus fruit. The Seville orange was the only orange available at that time and it was used in all recipes where oranges were required. Today we have a myriad different oranges to use, but the best marmalade is still made with Seville oranges.

Makes approx. 4kg/9½lb

1kg/2¼lb Seville oranges
1 lemon, unwaxed
1.75kg/4½lb preserving sugar

Wash and quarter the oranges and lemon. Remove the flesh, pips and pulp and tie in a muslin cloth. Slice the peel, finely or coarsely, whichever is preferred. Place the peel and the muslin bag in a preserving pan and pour on 2.2 litres/4 pints/9 cups water. Bring to the boil, then simmer for one and a half to two hours, until the peel is tender. Meanwhile, warm the sugar in the oven. Stir the sugar into the fruit until it is dissolved, then boil rapidly to setting point. Stand for 15 minutes. Pour the marmalade into warm, sterilized jars and seal.

Right: *Clockwise from top left: Orange marmalade, Rhubarb and mint jelly, Damson jam and Dried apricot jam.*

RHUBARB AND GINGER JAM

The best rhubarb for pies and tarts is the young, slender pink spring stems. Later in the summer, when the leaves have reached elephant-ear proportions and the stalks are thick and green, is the time to make this preserve. Use it with cream as a cake filling or stir it into plain yoghurt.

Makes approx. 2kg/4¾lb

1kg/2¼lb rhubarb
1kg/2¼lb preserving sugar
25g/1oz dried root ginger, bruised
115g/4oz crystallized ginger
50g/2oz candied orange peel, chopped

Cut the rhubarb into short pieces and layer with sugar in a glass bowl. Leave overnight. Put the rhubarb and dissolved sugar into a large preserving pan. Tie the bruised ginger root into a piece of muslin and add it to the rhubarb. Cook gently for 30 minutes until the rhubarb has softened. Then boil rapidly until the setting point is reached. Remove the muslin. Stir in the crystallized ginger and candied peel and leave for 15 minutes. Pour the jam into warm, dry, sterilized jars and seal.

LEMON AND LIME CURD

This sumptuously rich fruit curd is definitely not diet food, rather it is a treat to be brought out of the cupboard for a special tea time or as a particularly wonderful filling for a roulade.

Makes approx. 750g/1¾lb

3 large lemons, unwaxed
3 limes, unwaxed
175g/6oz unsalted butter
450g/1lb granulated sugar
4 large eggs, well beaten

1 *Wash the lemons and limes and finely grate the rinds.*

2 *Squeeze and then strain the juice of the lemons and limes.*

3 *Melt the butter in a double saucepan. Add the lemon rind, juice, sugar and well-beaten eggs. Cook the mixture over a gentle heat for about 25 minutes, stirring continuously until it is smooth and thick. Pour the curd into warm, sterilized jars and cover at once. Use within two months.*

Above: *Lemon and lime curd.*

Wash and pit the cherries and then pack them with the almonds into a sterilized, wide-necked bottle. Spoon the sugar over the fruit, then cover with the eau de vie and seal securely. Store for a month before using them, and shake the bottle every now and then to help dissolve the sugar.

SPICED PEARS

Similar to pickled pears, this conserve is for eating with cold meats. It is especially good with ham, pork or gammon.

Makes 1kg/2¼lb

600ml/1 pint/2½ cups red wine
  vinegar
rind of 1 lemon
4cm/1½ in piece fresh root ginger
1 cinnamon stick
2 tsp whole allspice berries
1 bay leaf
450g/1lb sugar
1kg/2¼lb hard pears
cloves

Above: *Spiced pears.*

Pour the vinegar into a saucepan, add the lemon rind, all the spices, except the cloves, and the bay leaf. Dissolve the sugar in the vinegar over a low heat. Peel the pears, leaving them whole, stick a clove into each one and add them to the vinegar. Simmer until the pears are tender and transparent. Lift them out and pack them into hot, sterilized jars. Boil the syrup until thickened and pour it over the pears, sealing immediately.

Bottled vegetables

With fresh vegetables available all the year round, we no longer need to rely on bottled vegetables in the way previous generations did, but they are still an excellent store cupboard standby, and with the addition of herbs and spices, are turned from a staple to a luxury item.

BOTTLED CHERRY TOMATOES

Cherry tomatoes bottled in their own juices with garlic and basil are sweetly delicious and a perfect accompaniment to thick slices of country ham.

Makes 1kg/2¼lb

1kg/2¼lb cherry tomatoes
1 tsp salt per 1 litre/1¾ pint/4 cup jar
1 tsp sugar per 1 litre/1¾ pint/4 cup jar
fresh basil
5 garlic cloves per jar

Above: *Bottled cherry tomatoes.*

1 *Prick each tomato with a toothpick.*

2 *Pack the tomatoes into clean dry jars, adding the salt and sugar as you go.*

3 *Fill the jars to within 2cm/¾in of the top, tuck the basil and garlic among the tomatoes. Rest the lids on the jars, but do not seal. Stand the jars on a baking tray lined with a layer of cardboard or newspaper in a low oven set at 120°C/250°F/Gas ½. After about 45 minutes, when the juice is simmering, remove the jars from the oven and seal. Store in a cool place and use within six months.*

PICKLED BEETROOT

Next time you decide to bake some potatoes, add a pan of beetroots to the oven and use them to make beetroot pickle, which will make a welcome change to the usual boiled variety – the flavour will be richer and earthier. If you are boiling the beetroots, cook them in their skins and leave them to cool in the cooking liquid and then gently rub off their skins. If you prefer, you can also use pre-cooked beetroot bought from the supermarket for this pickle.

Makes 450g/1lb

450g/1lb beetroot, cooked
1 large onion, sliced
300ml/½ pint/1¼ cups cider vinegar
50g/2oz sugar
few strips fresh horseradish (optional)

Slice the beetroot and pack it into a jar, layering it with the sliced onion. Pour the vinegar and 150ml/¼ pint/⅔ cup water into a saucepan. Add the sugar and horseradish (if using) and bring to the boil. Pour the liquid over the beetroot and seal the jar. Store in a cool place and use within one month, or longer if kept in the refrigerator.

PICKLED RED CABBAGE

This pickle is good served with bread and cheese or cold duck or goose.

Makes 1–1.5kg/2¼–3½lb

675g/1½lb shredded red cabbage
1 large Spanish onion, sliced

25g/1oz sea salt
600ml/1 pint/2½ cups red wine vinegar
75g/3oz brown sugar
1 tbsp coriander seeds
3 cloves
2.5cm/1in piece fresh root ginger
1 star anise
2 bay leaves
4 eating apples

Mix the cabbage and onion thoroughly with the salt, place in a colander and allow to drain overnight.

Rinse and take the excess water off the vegetables using a clean cloth. Pour the vinegar into a saucepan, add the sugar, spices and bay leaves. Bring to the boil then allow to cool.

Core and coarsely chop the apples and

Above: *Bottled young, succulent vegetables can be as delicious as freshly picked ones.*

then layer them with the cabbage and onions in clean, dry preserving jars. Pour on the cooled spiced vinegar (strain out the spices if you prefer a milder pickle), seal and store for a week before eating. Best eaten within two months.

Syrups, cordials and liqueurs

There is a freshness and intensity of flavour in home-made syrups, cordials and liqueurs that is very rarely present in their commercial counterparts. They will keep wonderfully from year to year in your store cupboard and may be used as flavourings for ice creams and sorbets as well as making delicious drinks.

ROSEHIP SYRUP

Rosehips are a rich source of vitamin C, so this is an ideal winter drink to ward off coughs and colds.

Makes approx. 750ml/1¼ pints/3 cups per 600ml/1 pint/2½ cups syrup
ripe but firm rosehips
granulated sugar

Wash the rosehips thoroughly, then top and tail. Place them in a food processor and chop coarsely. Tip them into a saucepan, barely cover with water and bring to the boil. Turn down the heat and leave to simmer gently for approximately ten minutes, until tender. Remove from the heat and then allow to stand for a further ten minutes. Leave to strain overnight through a thick jelly bag. The juice should be clear. However, if it is not, strain it through several thicknesses of muslin to remove any remaining particles. Measure the juice, and for each 600ml/1 pint/2½ cups, add 350g/12oz sugar. Boil until the syrup thickens and then pour into warm, dry, sterilized bottles and seal securely with a cork. To drink, dilute the syrup to taste with still or sparkling water.

ELDERFLOWER CORDIAL

The rather rank scent of the elderflower bush gives no clue to the delicate flavour of this cordial made from its flowers. It makes a wonderfully refreshing summer drink and a delicious sorbet. A spoonful of the cordial added to cooked gooseberries gives them a subtle muscatel flavour.

Makes 2.5 litres/4¼ pints/10¼ cups
1.5kg/3½lb granulated sugar
50g/2oz citric acid
25 elderflower heads, washed and
  gently shaken dry
2 lemons, unwaxed, sliced

Dissolve the sugar in 1.5 litres/2½ pints/6¼ cups hot water and leave to cool. When

Above: *Rosehip syrup and Elderflower cordial.*
Right: *Syrups and cordials are a delicious alternative to commercial squashes.*

cool, stir in the citric acid and add the elderflowers and sliced lemons. Cover and leave to infuse for two days, stirring occasionally. Strain and pour into clean, dry, sterilized bottles and seal. Store in a cool place to avoid the possibility of slight fermentation taking place. To serve, dilute to taste with still or sparkling mineral water. Will keep indefinitely in a cool place.

ELDERBERRY SYRUP

The elder bush is very generous with its bounty. Not only is it laden with foaming white flowers in the early summer, but it also hangs heavy with purple berries in the autumn. The berries are ripe when the heads hang down. Elderberry syrup is a traditional country treatment for coughs and colds.

Makes approx. 750ml/1¼ pints/3 cups per 600ml/1 pint/2½ cups syrup
ripe elderberries
granulated sugar
cinnamon sticks

Wash the heads of berries thoroughly, remove the stalks and then place the berries in a large earthenware pot. Cover and bake in a moderately hot oven at 190°C/375°F/Gas 5 until the juice runs. Strain off the juice into a saucepan, and for each 600ml/1 pint/2½ cups, add 225g/8oz sugar and a broken up stick of cinnamon. Cover the saucepan and boil gently until the syrup thickens. Pour the syrup into warm, dry, sterilized bottles and seal securely. To serve, just dilute to taste with hot water.

PEACH WINE

This is not really a proper wine at all, but instead a delicious and refreshing amalgam of peaches, wine and eau de vie. Although you could drink it at any time of the year, it is really intended to be made and drunk during the summer, either on its own or diluted with soda water.

Makes approx. 1.2 litres/2 pints/5 cups
6 ripe peaches
1 litre/1¾ pints/4 cups dry white wine
200g/7oz caster sugar
175ml/6fl oz/¾ cup eau de vie

1 *Peel and halve the peaches, then poach them in the white wine for approximately 15 minutes, until tender. Cover and allow to stand overnight.*

2 *Remove the peaches, then strain the liquid through a coffee filter. Add the sugar and eau de vie and stir to dissolve the sugar.*

3 *Pour the wine into clean, dry, sterilized bottles and cork. Store in the refrigerator. Drink within two weeks. Serve well chilled.*

Above: *Peach wine.*

MULBERRY RATAFIA

Ten years ago, I was lucky enough to have a glut of mulberries and I transformed some of the fruit into this delicious drink. There are still a couple of bottles left and the fresh mulberry taste has not diminished at all over the years.

Quantity depends on the amount of fruit picked
mulberries
caster sugar
vodka, brandy or gin

Fill clean, dry sterilized jars with clean fruit. Pour in caster sugar so that it comes a third of the way up the jar, then fill to the top with the spirit of your choice. Seal the jars and shake them to help the sugar dissolve. Store for at least a couple of months, occasionally shaking the jars.

Strain off the fruit (which you can use to make a delicious apple pie) and bottle the ratafia in clean, dry, sterilized bottles and seal securely. It should keep indefinitely if stored in airtight bottles.

SLOE GIN

This is a real country drink, which was traditionally used to celebrate high days and holidays. Sloes are gathered from the hedgerows after the first frosts and the first bottle is ready in time for Christmas.

Quantity depends on the amount of fruit picked
sloes
caster sugar
gin

Wash the sloes, removing any stalks, bits of twig or leaves. Prick each sloe with a toothpick or needle, then pack the fruit into a wide-necked jar or bottle. Pour in caster sugar so that it comes halfway up the jar, then fill to the top with gin and seal. Shake the jar from time to time to help the sugar dissolve. Before drinking, strain off the sloes and decant the sloe gin into a pretty bottle that is clean and dry.

Right: *Delicious and colourful liqueurs.*

Teas and tisanes

Before tea was widely available, country people made hot drinks from the herbs growing wild and in their gardens, and found them to be good for their health as well as pleasant tasting. With the arrival of teas from China, they followed the example of the Chinese and added flowers and other flavourings to enhance the taste and appearance of the teas.

ROSE PETAL TEA

Another delicious drink for summer, this one is very pretty when poured unstrained into tea glasses so that the petals and tea leaves are visible at the bottom of the glass.

Makes 130g/4½oz

15g/½oz scented red rose petals
115g/4oz Oolong tea

Mix the rose petals with the tea and store in an airtight container.

Above: *Marigold and verbena tisane.*

MARIGOLD AND VERBENA TISANE

This attractive and distinctive gold and green tisane is reputed to be excellent for purifying the blood and aiding digestion. Why not try drinking some after a heavy meal? The verbena gives the tea an intensely lemony flavour and the marigold adds a peppery note.

Makes 75g/3oz

50g/2oz dried marigold petals
25g/1oz dried lemon verbena leaves

Mix the petals and leaves together and then store in an airtight container. To serve, all you have to do is infuse one tablespoon of the tea in a mug of hot water, then leave it to stand, covered, for approximately five minutes before drinking.

Above: *Rose petal tea.*

ORANGE AND LEMON TEA

Citrus fruit adds a fresh zestiness to tea and this blend, with its addition of dried orange and lemon rind, is ideal for drinking without milk on a summer's afternoon. For an even more pronounced flavour, a few drops of orange and lemon essential oils can be mixed into the tea.

In a saucepan, mix the sugar and cream together until you have made a thick paste, then add the butter and chocolate and stir well. Place the mixture over a gentle heat and stir it until all the ingredients have completely melted and thoroughly blended. Then raise the heat and boil for five minutes while stirring constantly.

Finally, remove from the heat and beat the mixture until it is thick, then pour it into a previously buttered 20cm/8in square tin. Before the fudge has completely cooled, cut it into squares and place a half walnut on each square.

HOME-MADE TRUFFLES

Making truffles at home is easier than you think and can be great fun for all the family. However, they are fairly rich and are definitely something of a treat to be brought out on special occasions. They freeze very successfully.

Makes 20 truffles

225g/8oz plain chocolate
75g/3oz unsalted butter
1 egg yolk
cocoa powder for dusting

Above: *Home-made sweets may be a wicked indulgence in these health-conscious days, but everyone deserves a treat now and then.*

Break up the chocolate and melt it with the butter in a double boiler, stirring to make sure that they are thoroughly blended. Remove from the heat and stir in the egg yolk. Place the mixture in the refrigerator until it is firm enough to shape. Then roll the mixture into balls and roll these in the cocoa powder. Place each truffle in a paper case. Keep them in the refrigerator and use within one week.

The Bathroom

A selection of traditional creams, lotions and other natural beauty products to scent your bath and pamper your skin.

Making cosmetics

Cosmetics is another area of our modern life that we have handed over to the "experts". While it is true that many of today's products are more pleasing in texture and smell than earlier creams and lotions, it is also true that they are nearly all made from the same, easily obtainable basic ingredients and that we are paying more for the seductive packaging than for the contents. It can also be very rewarding using your own home-made creams and lotions. The simplest of the techniques in this section involves the mixing of like with like, for example diluting a herbal infusion with rosewater, or blending a carrier oil with essential oils.

CHOOSING AND USING SAFE INGREDIENTS
I have tried to ensure that all the ingredients in this section are readily available. Inevitably, some are harder to find than others, but your local pharmacist may be prepared to order these for you. Dried herbs can be bought by mail order (see list of suppliers, pages 156 and 157). When buying essential oils, it is very important that you purchase from companies with established reputations, as oils can vary enormously in quality. Although the ingredients in this section have been chosen with safety in mind, it is advisable to do a patch test with the cream or lotion before using it.

Left: *To test that your home-made cosmetics do not cause an allergic reaction, spread a small amount on your inner arm and leave for 24 hours to see whether there is an adverse reaction, such as a rash.*

WARNING: Certain essential oils should not be handled by pregnant women or anyone who may be pregnant or where there is an existing medical condition. If in any doubt, seek medical advice. Wear rubber gloves when handling the concentrated oil and spice blends to avoid any irritation.

TO MAKE A HERBAL INFUSION
Herbal infusions are very easy to make and are delicious to drink – either hot or cold. Always store them in a cool place or refrigerator. You can also make infusions from flowers. Mix these with rosewater or witch hazel to make soothing or refreshing skin tonics (see page 92).

25g/1oz dried herb or flower or 50g/2oz fresh herb or flower

1 *Place the herbs or flowers in a jug. If you prefer, you can mix the herbs or flowers together, but always ensure the total quantity remains the same in relation to the amount of water you use.*

2 *Pour 475ml/16fl oz/2 cups boiling water over the herbs or flowers. Cover with a lid or sterilized gauze and allow to cool at room temperature.*

3 *Strain the liquid into a sterilized bottle and seal. A jug with a tight-fitting lid would do. Store in the refrigerator and consume or use within two to three days.*

FLOWER OILS

The finest of the flower oils are listed below: rose, jasmine and neroli. As they are all quite costly, it may be impractical to buy them all; instead, why not choose your favourite and use it sparingly – a very little goes a long way.

Rose: Good rose oil can be bought in small quantities and is worth the investment for its incomparable fragrance and the fact that its gentle, soothing qualities make it particularly suitable for use in creams and lotions. Scented rose petals can be floated in a bath, or used to add colour and scent to bath salts and skin tonics.

Jasmine: A sensual and fragrant oil that lifts the spirits, jasmine oil is beneficial to older skins. Like rose petals, jasmine flowers can be used to scent a bath.

Neroli: Made from orange blossom, this essential oil is delicately fragrant and is also extensively used in perfumery. It induces a wonderful sense of well-being and relaxation.

Marigold: Although not used as an essential oil, this pretty garden flower's properties are used in creams for healing cuts and grazes (see page 110).

WOOD OILS

As the name suggests, these oils are derived from aromatic woods and have a resinous quality to them that is very attractive. Their fragrance is not overtly feminine and so they are suitable for use in oils and lotions for men.

Sandalwood: Sandalwood oil is used in skin-care products because it helps balance the production of the natural oils in the skin. It is useful in the treatment of acne and other skin conditions.

Cedarwood: Antiseptic and gently astringent, this oil helps in the treatment of skin conditions. However, it must not be used during pregnancy.

Frankincense: Made from a resin exuded by the bark of a shrubby tree, frankincense oil is excellent for use in creams and lotions for mature skins, and to treat any skin complaint.

Clockwise from top left: *Lavender, rosemary, chamomile, marigold, jasmine, rose, orange and lemon. Essential oils are traditionally extracted from herbs, fruit and flowers by one of three methods: distillation, extraction or expression. Although the scale and apparatus have altered over the centuries, the basic methods are the same.*

Massage oils and lotions

In the past, the country dweller would have balked at the idea of using massage oils and lotions, considering them far too hedonistic and time-wasting for hard-working folk, yet examination of the medicine cupboard would almost certainly have revealed a selection of liniments and embrocations for rubbing into stiff muscles. The names may have changed, but their purpose remains the same, and if we have now introduced more pleasure into the process, this is no bad thing. Indeed, what could be more pleasurable than a relaxing bath and a massage?

MIXING ESSENTIAL OILS

Make sure all containers are thoroughly cleaned and dry before mixing oils.

1 *Pour the base oil into a spotlessly clean and dry container.*

2 *Slowly add drops of essential oil into the container and mix thoroughly.*

Above: *The healing properties of marigolds have been known for centuries and the dried petals can be added to creams and lotions.*

MASSAGE OIL

Massage oils are a mixture of a base oil and aromatic essential oils. With the exception of lavender and ti-tree oils, essential oil should never be used undiluted on the skin. When making an oil for use on babies and small children, halve the quantity of essential oil in the recipe. A variety of base oils is available and if you are in any doubt, check for sensitivity with a patch test (see page 76). The vegetable and nut oils used in aromatherapy have been cold-pressed for this purpose, so do not be tempted to substitute ordinary cooking oils, which may well have had chemical stabilizers added to them. This recipe includes 10 % wheatgerm oil, which improves the keeping qualities of the massage oil and, being high in Vitamin E, makes it particularly good for the skin.

Makes 50ml/3½ tbsp

45ml/3 tbsp almond oil

5ml/1tsp wheatgerm oil

10 drops chamomile oil (for relaxation)

or

10 drops geranium oil (for gentle stimulation)

Pour the almond and wheatgerm oils into a glass bottle, add the essential oil of your choice and shake to mix. Store in a cool place away from the light.

TI-TREE MASSAGE LOTION

Ti-tree is one of the great healing oils, with wonderful antiseptic properties. It has a fresh, resinous smell, which makes it an ideal oil for use in a massage lotion for both men and women.

Makes 150ml/¼ pint/⅔ cup

½ tsp borax

7.5ml/½ tbsp white beeswax

45ml/3 tbsp coconut oil

30ml/2 tbsp almond oil

15ml/1 tbsp wheatgerm oil

20 drops ti-tree oil

Dissolve the borax in 60ml/4 tbsp boiled water. Melt the beeswax with the coconut, almond and wheatgerm oils in a double boiler over a gentle heat. Remove from the heat when completely melted and slowly pour in the borax solution, while stirring continuously with a whisk. The lotion will begin to emulsify (turn milky and thicken)

immediately. Continue to whisk until the mixture has cooled, then add the ti-tree oil. Pour the lotion into a glass bottle or jar, and preferably one that is coloured. Store the container in a cool place away from direct sunlight.

Above: *Plain glass bottles are ideal containers for storing your soothing massage lotions and oils. Bottles with glass stoppers were once used in pharmacies and copies of these are now readily available.*

LAVENDER BODY LOTION

This creamy lotion is perfect for treating dry skin in winter and can also be used to soothe sunburnt skin, as lavender oil is a very effective treatment for burns.

Makes 120ml/4fl oz/½ cup
¼ tsp borax
5ml/1tsp white beeswax
5ml/1tsp lanolin
30ml/2 tbsp petroleum jelly
25ml/5 tsp apricot kernel oil
20ml/4 tsp cold-pressed sunflower oil
20 drops lavender oil

1 *Dissolve the borax in 30ml/2 tbsp boiled water. Melt the beeswax, lanolin and petroleum jelly with the apricot kernel and cold-pressed sunflower oil in a double boiler. Remove from the heat once the wax has melted and stir well to blend.*

2 *Add the borax solution, whisking as you do so. The lotion will turn white and thicken but keep whisking until cool. Then stir in the lavender oil. Pour into a glass jar or bottle and store in a cool, dark place.*

Above: *Lavender is a popular herb to grow.*

PEPPERMINT BODY LOTION

This lotion is made as for the lavender body lotion, but using only 10 drops of peppermint oil. Use this refreshing and invigorating lotion after hard physical work. Do not use on small children or during pregnancy.

LAVENDER BUBBLE BATH

There is no need to buy commercially made bubble baths again. This bubble bath is quite delicious and so simple to make that you can prepare some extra as gifts for friends and family.

Makes 1 bottle
bunch lavender
1 large bottle clear organic shampoo
5 drops lavender oil

Place the bunch of lavender head down in a clean, wide-necked screw-top jar. You only really need the flowers, so cut off any long stalks. Add the shampoo and the lavender oil. Close the jar and place it on a sunny windowsill for two to three weeks, shaking occasionally. Strain the liquid and re-bottle.

HERBAL BATH BAGS

Hang from the bath tap and run hot water through these herbal bags to release lovely relaxing scents.

Makes 3 bags
three 23cm/9in diameter muslin circles
6 tbsp bran
1 tbsp lavender flowers
1 tbsp chamomile flowers
1 tbsp rosemary tips
3 small rubber bands
3m/3yd narrow ribbon or twine

Place two tablespoons of bran in the centre of each circle of muslin. Add lavender to one, chamomile to a second and rosemary to a third. Gather the material up, close with a rubber band and tie with ribbon.

Right: *Lavender body lotion.*

Nourishing creams

The countrywoman has always known the value of protecting her skin, and these creams provide excellent protection.

TRADITIONAL COLD CREAM

This is an all-purpose cream that can be used to cleanse and soothe the skin.

Makes 200g/7oz

50g/2oz white beeswax

115g/4oz almond oil

½ tsp borax

50ml/2fl oz/¼ cup rosewater

1 Place the beeswax in a double boiler and add the almond oil. Melt the wax over a gentle heat, stirring all the time to combine the ingredients.

2 Take off the heat and dissolve the borax in the rosewater. Slowly pour it into the melted wax and oil, whisking all the time.

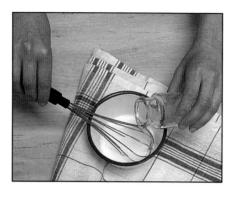

3 It will quickly turn milky and thicken. Continue whisking while it cools. When it reaches thick pouring consistency, pour into glass or china pots.

Above: *Traditional cold cream.*

ROSE-SCENTED MOISTURE CREAM

Rich in nourishing oils and waxes, this moisturizer is a highly effective night cream. If you have difficulty obtaining emulsifying wax, however, use white beeswax instead.

Makes approx. 175ml/6fl oz/¾ cup

120ml/4fl oz/½ cup rosewater

½ tsp glycerine

30ml/2 tbsp witch hazel

¼ tsp borax

30ml/2 tbsp emulsifying wax or white beeswax

5ml/1 tsp lanolin

30ml/2 tbsp almond oil

2 drops rose oil

Gently heat the rosewater, glycerine, witch hazel and borax in a saucepan until the borax has dissolved. In a double boiler, melt the wax, lanolin and almond oil over a gentle heat. Slowly add the rosewater mixture to the oil mixture, whisking as you do so. It will quickly turn milky and thicken. Take off the heat, continue to whisk as it cools, and then add the rose oil. Pour the cream into china or glass pots.

UNSCENTED MOISTURE CREAM

Ideal for applying before going outdoors, this simple, unscented cream can be used by both men and women.

Makes approx. 150ml/¼ pint/⅔ cup

30ml/2 tbsp carnauba wax

15ml/1 tbsp white beeswax

120ml/4fl oz/½ cup almond oil

Melt the waxes and oil in a double boiler over a gentle heat and stir. Take off the heat and pour the cream into a pot to set.

Right: *Antique pots containing creams.*

Cleansers and skin tonics

Exfoliating washing grains, flower skin tonics and gentle cleansers can be made at home for a fraction of the cost of many commercial products, and if kept in pretty bottles and jars, will look just as attractive on the dressing table.

ALMOND OIL CLEANSER

This gentle cleanser will leave the skin feeling soft and supple.

Makes approx. 400ml/14fl oz/1⅔ cups
50g/2oz white beeswax
300ml/½ pint/1¼ cups almond oil
120ml/4fl oz/½ cup rosewater
½ tsp borax
4 drops rose oil (optional)

Melt the beeswax in a double boiler over a gentle heat and slowly add the almond oil. Slightly warm the rosewater and dissolve the borax in it. Pour the rosewater into the oil mixture, whisking all the time as it emulsifies. Take off the heat and keep whisking as it cools. Add the rose oil if required. Pour into glass pots or jars.

ORANGE AND OATMEAL WASHING GRAINS

If you like to wash your face, rather than use cleansers, this is a marvellous once-a-week treatment to exfoliate the skin and leave it feeling soft and glowing. Use the peel of organic oranges because they will not have been sprayed with chemicals or waxes. To use the grains,

Above: *Orangeflower and cornflower tonics.*

place a teaspoonful in the palm of the hand, mix to a paste with water and rub gently into the skin; rinse off and dry.

2 tbsp fine oatmeal
1 tbsp ground orange peel

Mix the two ingredients and keep in a lidded bowl or jar in the bathroom.

SKIN TONICS

Different formulations of skin tonics are used to soothe or stimulate the skin. Fine dry skins need soothing with delicate herbal infusions or flower waters, while large-pored or oily skins can benefit from a stimulating tonic containing witch hazel.

Skin tonics are made by pouring the ingredients into a glass bottle and shaking to mix. To use, pour a little on to a dampened piece of cotton wool.

Each recipe makes 100ml/6½ tbsp

Orangeflower Skin Tonic
(normal skin)
75ml/5 tbsp orangeflower water
25ml/1½ tbsp rosewater

Cornflower Skin Tonic
(normal skin)
75ml/5 tbsp cornflower infusion
  (see page 110)
25ml/1½ tbsp rosewater

Elderflower Skin Tonic
(dry skin)
50ml/3¼ tbsp elderflower infusion
  (see page 76)
50ml/3¼ tbsp rosewater

Lavender Skin Tonic
(oily skin)
75ml/5 tbsp lavender infusion
  (see page 76)
25ml/1½ tbsp witch hazel

Linden Skin Tonic
(for mature skin)
90ml/4¾ tbsp limeflower infusion
  (see page 76)
10ml/1¾ tsp rosewater

Right: *The natural way – simple cosmetics made with pure ingredients.*

Makes 1.2 litres/2 pints/5 cups
50g/2oz sprigs of rosemary
300ml/½ pint/1¼ cups cider vinegar
10 drops rosemary oil

Pour 900ml/1½ pints/3¾ cups boiling water over the rosemary sprigs, cover and leave to infuse overnight. Strain the liquid, add the vinegar and the essential oil, then pour into a stoppered bottle.

OIL TREATMENT FOR HAIR

Hair that is regularly exposed to the elements can become dry and unmanageable. An oil treatment once a month will work wonders for your hair and scalp. Use the oil sparingly on dry hair. Coat the hair rather than saturate it, and gently massage it in. Cover with a hot towel for 20 minutes, then shampoo off.

Above: *Herbal hair treatments restore shine to your hair and improve scalp condition.*

Makes 4–6 treatments
90ml/6 tbsp coconut oil
3 drops rosemary oil
2 drops ti-tree oil
2 drops lavender oil

Blend and store in dark-coloured bottles.

The Still Room

Tempting ideas for scenting and decorating your home,
natural remedies and other recipes from the still room.

The history of the still room

In Tudor times, in the sixteenth century, the still room could be described as the control centre of the domestic economy. It was here that the countrywoman would store her precious herbs and spices, and make lotions, potions and distillations. In doing so, she could be described as the family doctor, pharmacist, herbalist, perfumer, candlemaker and pest controller all rolled into one, and the health and well-being of everyone in the household was her responsibility.

Her knowledge was of a very practical nature, based on skill, observation and recipes passed from generation to generation. Her day, her week, her year were full of myriad tasks which had to be completed to keep her home running efficiently, and it is not surprising that few had the time, energy or learning to write down their recipes and formulae. From the manuscripts that do survive, it is clear that these women were full of common sense and a real understanding of the materials they worked with, apparently in marked contrast to the herbalists and doctors of the time who were much inclined to invoke magical powers and use disgusting and dangerous ingredients in their cures.

Nowadays, potpourris, flower waters and scented candles are pleasing decorative accessories, but in the Tudor household they were essential to ward off dreadful odours and keep pests and disease at bay. Indeed, the scents they used were far from subtle.

Herbs were gathered, dried, stored and used in large quantities to add savour to food and disguise the less than fresh taste of most meat as well as for numerous medicinal infusions, distillations and for strewing underfoot.

Spices were precious commodities, carefully guarded by the housewife who would keep them under lock and key and closely supervise their use. Although expensive, they were used in huge amounts: we would find these quantities quite overpowering, but like herbs, they were a disguise for rancid flavours. Their curative powers were also well recognized and respected.

The modern still room projects are, in many ways, highly romanticized versions of their medieval equivalents. We make these things for pleasure rather than for practical purposes, nevertheless they are fragrant, decorative and sometimes functional. By passing on these methods, we help to continue a tradition that has been an essential part of country life for centuries.

Left: *Fragrant and colourful dried flowers are stored in glass jars ready to be blended with herbs, spices and fixatives to make aromatic potpourris which can be used throughout the home.*

Natural remedies and medicines

In the past, the ability to treat effectively family coughs and colds, cuts and scratches was of vital importance to the country housewife, and she would pride herself on her knowledge and the array of lotions, ointments and infusions she kept in her still-room. The plants and herbs used then still grow wild in some of our fields and hedgerows, but few of us have the time and certainly not the knowledge to concoct the numerous cures and treatments which made up her pharmacy. Nevertheless, there are some old-fashioned remedies which we can easily and safely use.

Honey and lemon is a tried and trusted remedy for most sore throats. To make it, mix the juice of a large lemon with 1 tbsp of clear honey (or more, according to taste) and dilute with boiling water to make a wonderfully soothing hot drink.

Peppermint tea is a safe and palatable cure for indigestion and nausea.

Chamomile tea will calm restless children and ensure a good night's sleep for children and grown-ups alike.

Sage and honey tea is a comforting treatment for colds, coughs and sore throats. Add 15g/½oz sage leaves to 1 tbsp clear honey and the juice of a lemon, then dilute with 300ml/½ pint/1¼ cups boiling water. Cover and leave to infuse for about 20–30 minutes. Strain and serve hot.

Calendula (marigold) cream is still popular as a treatment for cuts and scratches. To obtain an extract of marigold, tightly pack the flower heads into a wide-necked jar, close and leave on a sunny windowsill for seven to ten days. Strain off the oily sediment that forms at the bottom of the bottle. Substitute this extract for the essential oil in the healing ointment recipe (see page 94). Apply the cream to minor cuts and sores.

Witch hazel dabbed on to bites and stings will relieve the pain.

Cornflower infusion soothes tired and sore eyes. Infuse 2 tbsp cornflower flowers in 120ml/4fl oz/½ cup water. Cover and leave to cool. Strain and soak cotton wool pads with the infusion. Leave on the eyelids for 15 minutes.

Garlic is a powerful, if somewhat smelly, antiseptic. Taken regularly in food it purifies the blood and lowers cholesterol.

Rosehip and hibiscus tea is a rich source of vitamin C and will help keep coughs and colds at bay.

Elderflower and peppermint tea taken early will relieve feverishness.

Rosewater or orangeflower water added in very small amounts to hot water can be drunk daily to keep the skin clear and soothe the digestion. Only culinary-quality flower waters should be used in this way.

Left: *Healing herbs and flowers kept in the compartments of an old stone dish.*

Right: *Simple home remedies can be used to help treat minor complaints such as a cold.*

Scented polishes

Old-fashioned polishes are coming back into favour as we discover that spray polishes seldom give furniture the deep, glowing shine of a natural wax polish.

BEESWAX AND TURPENTINE POLISH

This is a very simple polish to make and the addition of wood oils will give it an attractive resinous fragrance. Lemon or lavender essential oil may also be used in this polish. Apply the polish to your furniture using a soft cloth, leave a few minutes to dry, then buff vigorously with a soft duster to achieve a deep, lustrous shine.

Makes 250ml/8fl oz/1 cup
75g/3oz natural beeswax
200ml/7fl oz/¾ cup pure turpentine
20 drops cedarwood oil
10 drops sandalwood oil

Above: *Beeswax and linseed oil.*

1 *Grate the beeswax coarsely and place in a screw-top jar.*

2 *Pour on the turpentine, screw on the lid and leave for a week, stirring occasionally until the mixture becomes a smooth cream. Add the essential oils and mix them in well. The polish is then ready to use.*

FURNITURE REVIVER

Wooden surfaces can become grimy from a combination of dirt and a build-up of spray polish. Use this traditional country recipe to loosen the grime and feed the wood at the same time. It works best if it is used over a few weeks, as it will gradually remove the layers of polish and, once the surface is cleaned, you can return to a conventional furniture polish. Apply with a soft cloth, leave for a few minutes, then wipe off with a second cloth.

Makes 750ml/1¼ pints/3 cups
250ml/8fl oz/1 cup malt vinegar
250ml/8fl oz/1 cup pure turpentine
250ml/8fl oz/1 cup raw linseed oil
1 tbsp granulated sugar

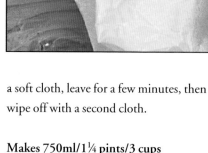

Measure all the ingredients into a bottle with a cork or screw top, seal and shake well to mix. Label the bottle clearly.

CLEANING VINEGARS

Malt vinegar is an extremely versatile and effective household cleaner, especially in areas where limescale from hard water is a problem. At its simplest, vinegar can be used undiluted to give a brilliant clarity to newly cleaned windows. Wipe over the window with a cloth or sponge dipped in vinegar and then polish dry with a crumpled piece of newspaper – this is an old but reliable way of achieving sparkling windows. Similarly, keep a spray bottle of

Above: *A selection of traditional cloths, brushes and polishes stands ready for spring cleaning treasured pieces of furniture.*

vinegar in the bathroom and use it to keep shower screens free of water marks and prevent the build up of limescale on tiles, baths and basins.

Rolled beeswax candles

Candles made from sheets of beeswax are very easy to make, beautiful to look at and aromatic to burn. Good-quality beeswax retains a strong scent of honey and the sweet smell will fill the room when the candles are lit. The wax should be at room temperature before rolling, otherwise it may be difficult to work with. A hairdryer set at a low temperature will help soften the wax without melting it.

Makes one candle
23cm/9in length of wick
20 x 35cm/8 x 13¾in sheet of beeswax
melted beeswax for brushing
paintbrush

Above: *A fragrant beeswax candle.*

1 *Lay the wick across the width of the beeswax sheet and cut it to length.*

2 *Gently fold the wax over the wick and roll the sheet into a cylinder.*

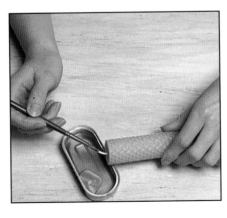

3 *Prime the protruding wick by brushing it with melted wax.*

SCENTED CANDLES

Candles that look beautiful and smell wonderful are my favourite way of scenting a room. When making them, essential oils can be used singly or combined to create the fragrance of your choice. Old terracotta pots make simple but good-looking moulds for the candles and can be used again and again. Scent with flower oils for a candlelit dinner, citronella or rosemary to keep insects at bay on a summer's evening and frankincense for festivals.

Fills one 10cm/4in pot
small piece of putty or clay
115g/4oz paraffin wax
25g/1oz beeswax
15cm/6in of 18mm/¾in wick
25 drops essential oil

Block the hole in the base of the pot with the putty or clay. Melt the paraffin and beeswax together in a double boiler over a gentle heat. Add the essential oil.

Dip the wick into the melted wax, then push the end of the wick into the clay or putty and position it centrally in the pot. Pour the melted wax into the pot. Drape the end of the wick over a spoon handle or stick laid on the rim of the pot to hold it in its central position while the wax sets. As the wax cools, a dip will form around the wick. Fill this with more wax if you wish.

Right: *The soft glow of candlelight is flattering and relaxing, and if you have a good stock of candles, you can easily create a mysterious and romantic ambience.*

Garlands and swags

As the seasons change, so do the flowers and natural decorations in the country home: the daffodils and bluebells of spring; the cow parsley and dog-roses of summer; and the brightly coloured berries of autumn. Other natural decorations also make their way indoors: autumn leaves gathered while walking down the lane and brought indoors as precious treasures, an abandoned bird's nest found in a winter hedgerow or a basket of pine cones picked in the woods.

A MOSS AND TWIG GARLAND

Mosses and lichens are the predominant materials for this garland, with twigs, cones and golden mushrooms adding the finishing touches. I pick up fallen twigs and cones when I am out for walks but I buy all the other materials from good dried flower suppliers, and so should you unless you have a plentiful supply available on your own land. When working with carpet moss it should be torn rather than cut to ensure that pieces join up in a natural-looking way.

florist's wire
30cm/12in straw ring
selection of mosses such as carpet moss, oak-
*   moss, spanish moss, reindeer moss and bun*
*   moss, all used here*
German pins or pins made from bent
*   florist's wire*
glue gun and glue sticks
small cones
golden mushrooms
twigs

1 *Attach a loop of wire to the back of the wreath. Cover the ring with carpet moss, pinning it as you go, until covered. Start to position the other mosses, also pinning them.*

2 *Alternatively, glue the other mosses in place using a glue gun. When all the mosses are in place, add the cones, mushrooms and twigs.*

3 *Fasten the cones together by twisting a piece of wire in between the layers of scales at the base of each cone. Apply some glue to the base of the cones before pinning them in place.*

4 *Glue the mushrooms in position and use pins to fasten small groups of twigs to the garland.*

A HERB GARLAND

A length of twiggy vine that has been twist-ed into a circle and tied in shape makes the base of this garland. Bunches of herbs are then tied to the ring with string to allow the herbs to be removed for use in cooking. Remember though that herbs exposed to direct sunlight and dust will not be as aromatic and tasty as those that have been stored in sealed jars in the store cupboard.

Above: *A herb garland.*
Right: *A garland of moss, twigs and cones.*

Above: *A spicy garland.*

A BAY LEAF RING

This is a lovely way to store your bay leaves. The ring below makes a simple decoration and the bay leaves are always readily to hand. The fresh leaves are threaded on to plastic-coated garden wire which is twisted into a circle and decorated with a raffia bow.

Above: *A bay leaf ring.*

A SPICY GARLAND

To make this colourful and flavourful garland, galvanized wire is shaped into a circle (coat hanger wire is ideal) and the chillis and orange rind are threaded on. The chillis and orange rind can be broken off to use in cooking or the garland can be treated purely as a decorative object.

A HOP AND HYDRANGEA SWAG

In the autumn the hop bines are harvested for use in the brewing industry. They dry most attractively and can also be used to make beautiful natural swags to decorate beams or the tops of cupboards and

dressers. During the year their colour will fade, so that by the following autumn, you will be ready to take them down and replace them with the new season's hops. Hop bines are quite brittle so it is advisable to spray them with water and leave them to moisten overnight before you work with them. They can simply be pinned in place or tied to sisal rope as they have been for this swag, which has been decorated with bunches of hydrangeas tied on with hessian bows. Poppy seedheads, pink rosebuds and pink peppercorns add a touch of colour.

Right: *A hop bine decorated with hydrangeas, roses, berries and poppy seedheads.*

Seasonal Celebrations

Ideas and inspirations for recipes and decorations to enhance country festivals throughout the year.

The passing seasons

In the countryside the passing of the year has always been marked with festivals and celebrations. From earliest times, when these rites were ceremonies of invocation and offerings to the gods – to ensure that the sun returned after the long winter, that the rain fell in spring and that the harvest was bounteous and safely gathered in – the country dweller has remained in close touch with the seasons, aware that each month brings its allotted tasks and that time must be used wisely and well if all is to be completed.

The major festivals we celebrate today are a mixture of those early pagan rites and celebrations with Christian religious ceremony, brought about when the priests, realizing they could not suppress the old ways, decided to incorporate elements of the old festivals into the major Christian festivals.

However we decide to mark these festivals, whether in a religious or secular manner, there is a deeply instinctive need to acknowledge and celebrate seasonal changes. Few of us are untouched by the arrival of spring, the extraordinary emergence of new life from what seems a cold, unwelcoming environment. Within weeks, what was bare brown earth is a carpet of colour as young plants race into lush growth and flower with almost indecent haste. No wonder the priests looked for a serious ceremony to put the lid on all this rising sap and rampant reproduction. In Christianity the weeks leading up to Easter are intended as a time of self-denial and reflection, but the

Above: *Summer celebrations are marked by outdoor meals deliciously flavoured with intensely aromatic fresh herbs, which grow prolifically in this season of warm abundance.*

culmination is a glorious celebration of resurrection and what more appropriate time than spring when the evidence of returning life is all around.

Nowadays, few of us celebrate May Day or Midsummer's Day as would have been done by country people in the past. Instead, we save the summer months for more personal celebrations such as family christenings, weddings or that institution unknown to our forebears, the annual summer holiday.

The coming of autumn brings the Harvest Festival, which in the country has real meaning and significance. There is a great feeling of relief and achievement when the last of the corn is harvested, when hay and straw are baled and stacked and the crops are lifted. Even the city dweller cannot fail to notice that the market stalls and super-market shelves are a rich kaleidoscope of sun-ripened produce and the most urban of schools will use this festival as an opportunity to introduce children to the circle of the seasons. In North America, Thanksgiving Day has its origins in harvest festivals, but is now celebrated separately as a national day of thanksgiving and is a time

Left: *The first spring flowers mean that life is returning to the country. With their vibrant colours and heady aromas, they herald the return of sunshine and blue skies after the long, dark winter.*

when far-flung families make an effort to come together, renew ties and share a celebratory meal.

Halloween is the one festival still celebrated today that is predominantly pagan. Its origins are druidic and, though it was given Christian status as All Saints Night, it is generally thought of as the night when the dead are supposed to return as ghosts to make mischief. Its mix of fear and fun is irresistible to children.

The onset of winter, with its short days and long nights, would be a difficult time to endure if it were not for the anticipation of Christmas. At the darkest time of year, we celebrate a festival of blazing fires, good cheer, good food and good company. For country people it is a time when good husbandry in the earlier months allows time for socializing and relaxing, a welcome break from the hard work of every day, when each of us celebrates in our own way the passing of the old year and the coming of the new.

Above: *The pears, crab apples and other fruit that are harvested in the autumn and stored in the store cupboard hold deep within them the delicious flavour and glowing colour of summer sunshine.*

Right: *The evocative and powerfully resinous scent of pine branches and fir cones slowly spreads through the house as preparations are underway for the coming Christmas festivities.*

Easter

Easter eggs and the Easter rabbit are both pre-Christian symbols of fertility which have survived into the festival we celebrate today. In some country areas, the tradition of rolling dyed eggs down a hill still survives and it is variously attributed to symbolizing the returning sun or rolling away the stone from Christ's tomb.

SIMNEL CAKE

Halfway through Lent, it was the custom to make a simnel cake which would be brought out to celebrate Easter Day and the end of the lenten fast. I cannot say that I remember our family fasting during Lent, but we did enjoy my mother's simnel cake, which was part of our Easter celebrations, along with those other traditional Easter treats, hot cross buns.

Serves 8–12

225g/8oz plain flour
pinch of salt
115g/4oz sultanas
50g/2oz chopped almonds
50g/2oz chopped walnuts
40g/1½oz candied peel
grated rind of half a lemon
75g/3oz crystallized ginger, chopped
175g/6oz glacé cherries, quartered
200g/7oz butter
175g/6oz caster sugar
4 eggs
5ml/1tsp vanilla essence
30ml/2 tbsp brandy
apricot jam, sieved, for brushing
500g/1lb 2oz marzipan
food dye for colouring (optional)

Above: *Simnel cake.*

Preheat the oven to 160°C/325°F/Gas 3. Sift the flour and salt together into a bowl. Add the sultanas, nuts, candied peel, lemon rind, ginger and cherries and mix until everything is coated with the flour.

Cream the butter with the sugar until soft. Beat in the eggs one at a time, then add the vanilla essence. Gradually stir in the flour and fruit mixture, adding the brandy with the last of the flour. Pour into a lined 20cm/8in diameter cake tin and bake for one hour, then for another hour at 150°C/300°F/Gas 2.

Allow the cake to cool before storing it in a tin for four to six days before decorating. To decorate the cake, brush over with sieved apricot jam, before rolling out the marzipan and cutting it to fit the cake. Decorate the edge of the cake with a marzipan plait and the centre with marzipan eggs coloured with a little food dye.

Right: *A feast for Easter day.*

PUMPKIN FRITTERS

These moist and delicious fritters should
be eaten while still hot, liberally sprinkled
with cinnamon sugar.

Makes 16–20

75g/3oz sultanas
brandy (optional)
450g/1lb pumpkin, cooked and drained
50g/2oz plain flour, sifted twice
1 tbsp demerara sugar
½ tsp baking powder
pinch of salt
rind of 1 lemon
oil for frying

Soak the sultanas in warm water or brandy
for about 15 minutes, then drain well.
Place the pumpkin, flour, sugar, baking
powder, salt and lemon rind in a food
processor and blend until the mixture is
smooth. Stir in the sultanas, mixing lightly
to incorporate air into the batter. Heat the
oil in a frying pan and drop walnut-sized
balls of the mixture into the oil. Cook
briefly, turning once, until the fritters are
lightly browned.

Above: *The Halloween feast – a laden table
lit by glowing candles and lanterns.*

133

Harvest and Thanksgiving

In the New World, Thanksgiving has superceded the traditional Harvest Festival, which is still celebrated in Europe. Many of the trappings and symbols of the two festivals are very similar. Central to both celebrations is the giving of thanks for the safe gathering in of the harvest.

A DECORATIVE WHEATSHEAF

In pagan times, a miniature stook of wheat in the home would have been an offering to the gods; now it is simply an attractive country decoration. Traditionally, the farmer's family would make a corn dolly, a plaited decoration, from the last sheaf of wheat to be gathered in and this would be brought indoors for the harvest supper and kept in the farmhouse until the next harvest. Many of the corn dollies were extremely elaborate and each family had

Above: *A flat-backed tin container of wheat.*

its own designs. This wheatsheaf is not difficult to make but does require a little patience to achieve a good result. It is made using bunches of wheat bought from a dried flower supplier.

4 bunches wheat
silver birch twigs
string

Undo one bunch of wheat and adjust the heads so that they are level with one another. Once you are satisfied with what you have done, firmly tie the bunch together halfway down the stems. Repeat with two more of the bunches then tie the three completed bunches into one large bunch. Use the remaining bunch of wheat as the outer layer of the wheatsheaf and tie it in place. Trim the base of the stems level so that the sheaf will stand upright. Twist the silver birch twigs into and around the wheatsheaf and tie them in place.

HEART OF WHEAT

Fashion a heart at harvest time, when wheat is plentiful, for a delightful decoration that would look good adorning a wall or a dresser at any time of the year. Despite its delicate feathery appearance, this heart is quite robust and should last many years.

scissors
heavy-gauge garden wire, or similar
florist's tape
florist's wire
large bundle of wheat ears

Above: *Heart of wheat.*

Cut three long lengths of heavy-gauge wire and bend them into a heart shape. Twist the ends together at the bottom. Bind the wire heart shape with florist's tape. Using florist's wire, make enough small bundles of wheat ears to cover the wire heart shape densely. Leave a short length of wire at each end for fixing to the heart shape. Starting at the bottom, tape the first bundle of wheat ears to the heart. Place the second bundle farther up the heart shape behind the first, and tape it in position. Alternate the angle of the bundle of wheat as you work. Continue until the whole heart is covered. For the bottom, wire together about six bunches of wheat ears, twist the wires together and wire them to the heart, finishing off with florist's tape to neaten.

Right: *An attractive sculptural wheatsheaf bound with silver birch twigs.*

THE HARVEST LOAF

The harvest loaf is traditionally displayed at the altar amongst the fruit and vegetables and other offerings from the people of the parish. In the past there used to be fierce rivalry between neighbouring parishes as they tried to outdo one another with the intricacy and skill of their designs. Although there were many different designs of harvest loaf, the most enduringly popular was the wheatsheaf, symbolic as it is of the harvest and the vital importance of bread as "the staff of life".

Above: *The harvest loaf is in two parts joined by the plaited binding.*

Makes two 750g/1¾lb loaves

1.5kg/3½lb strong white flour

6 tsp salt

15g/½oz dried yeast

sugar, to activate yeast

egg, beaten, to glaze

Sift the flour and salt together into a bowl and make a well. Mix the yeast with 105ml/7 tbsp warm water and a little sugar and leave to activate for 15 minutes. Add the yeast mixture and 750ml/1¼ pints/3 cups water to the flour and mix thoroughly using your hands. Turn out on to a floured surface and knead until the dough becomes elastic. Place the dough in a lightly oiled bowl, cover and leave to prove for one to two hours, until it has doubled in size. Preheat the oven to 220°C/425°F/Gas 7. The high salt content in the dough makes it easier to work, but as food the bread is more decorative than palatable.

TO FORM THE LOAF

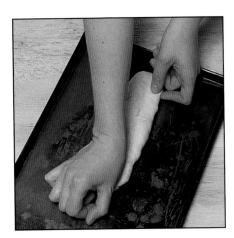

1 *Take approximately 225g/8oz of the dough and roll it into a 30cm/12in long cylinder. Place it on a large oiled and floured baking sheet and flatten slightly with your hand. This will form the long body of the bread, symbolizing the long stalks of the wheatsheaf.*

2 *Take about 350g/12oz of the remaining dough, roll and shape it into a crescent and place this at the top of the cylinder and flatten. Divide the remaining dough in half. Take one half and divide it in two again. Use one half to make the stalks of the wheat by rolling into narrow ropes and placing on the "stalk" of the sheaf. Use the other half to make a plait to decorate the finished loaf where the stalks meet the ears of wheat.*

3 *Use the remaining dough to make the ears of wheat. Roll it into small sausage shapes and snip each a few times with scissors to give the effect of the separate ears. Place these on the crescent shape, fanning out from the base until the wheatsheaf is complete. Position the plait between the stalks and the ears of wheat. Brush the wheatsheaf with the beaten egg. Bake for 20 minutes, then reduce the heat to 160°C/325°F/Gas 3 and bake for a further 20 minutes.*

Right: *The harvest loaf.*

HERBED CORNBREAD

Cornbread is a delicious, moist, cake-like bread that is served at Thanksgiving in recognition of the importance of the maize harvest to the American people. This herbed cornbread, made with herbs of your choice, is a delicious variation that deserves to be eaten more than once a year.

Makes 16 x 5cm/2in squares

165g/5½oz plain flour
125g/4½oz yellow cornmeal
65g/2½oz sugar
1 tbsp baking powder
¾ tsp salt
250ml/8fl oz/1 cup milk
1 large egg
2 tbsp unsalted butter, melted and cooled
2 tbsp finely chopped fresh herbs

Preheat the oven to 220°C/425°F/Gas 7. Sift all the dry ingredients together into a bowl. In another bowl beat together the milk, egg, butter and herbs. Stir the liquid ingredients into the dry ones until just combined. Pour the batter into a buttered 20cm/8in square tin. Bake the cornbread for 15 minutes until it is puffed and golden. Using a skewer, check that the centre is cooked. Cut into squares and serve warm with butter.

Above: *Squares of herbed cornbread.*

CRANBERRY, SULTANA AND WALNUT TART

This is an ideal dessert for anyone who is not madly keen on cranberries but feels that they are an essential part of the celebration and should feature at some stage.

Serves 6–8

225g/8oz fresh cranberries
250g/9oz sultanas
115g/4oz chopped walnuts
115g/4oz demerara sugar
50ml/2fl oz/¼ cup maple syrup
15ml/1 tbsp brandy
grated rind of 1 orange
25cm/10in flan tin lined with shortcrust pastry, chilled
25g/1oz cold unsalted butter, cubed

Preheat the oven to 220°C/425°F/Gas 7 and preheat a baking sheet. Place the cranberries and sultanas in a bowl and mix well. Add the remaining ingredients, except the butter, and toss so that the cranberries, nuts and sultanas are coated. Pour the mixture into the prepared pastry case and dot the surface with the butter. Place on the preheated baking sheet and bake for about 15 minutes, then reduce the heat to 180°C/350°F/Gas 4 and bake for 30 minutes.

CRANBERRY AND ORANGE SAUCE

Cranberries are also from the New World and this sauce, which accompanies the Thanksgiving turkey, has also become an essential part of Christmas dinner.

Above: *Orange zest is one of the flavourings in the cranberry, sultana and walnut tart.*

Makes 500g/1lb 2oz

225g/8oz cranberries
175ml/6fl oz/¾ cup fresh orange juice
115g/4oz sugar
30ml/2 tbsp Grand Marnier
1 tsp grated orange rind

Cook the cranberries in the orange juice until they are soft; this should take approximately five minutes. Then remove them from the heat and add the remaining ingredients. Finally, spoon the sauce into clean, dry jars and cover. Keep the sauce in the refrigerator until used.

It is vitally important to make sure that you do not overcook this sauce, which it is quite easy to do if you are not careful, because the cranberries will then develop a rather unpleasant bitter taste.

Right: *The larder's shelves are groaning with delicious Thanksgiving food.*

Christmas

Most of us are nostalgic for the traditional country Christmas, even if we have lived all our lives in the city; each year we optimistically think this year's festivities will be the perfect Christmas – and just occasionally it is. A laden table will appear with no dramas in the kitchen or harassed cooks, the tree will look magical, the relatives will all love one another and the children will be filled with rosy-cheeked wonder. One of the secrets of an enjoyable Christmas is not to try to do it all. Christmas should be a celebration for everyone, even the organizer, and a few things done well will give more pleasure than tired and resentful hosts.

Above: *Cones and seedheads for the garland.*

A CHRISTMAS GARLAND

A colourful, welcoming garland on the door sets the scene for Christmas. The natural materials create a wonderful texture and wired ribbon will be able to stand up to all but the most extreme of weather conditions. The coarse sisal rope bows make an interesting contrast to the luxurious bows.

1 *Use a length of wire to attach a small loop to the straw ring to allow you to hang the garland. Cover the ring with carpet moss, pinning it in place with the German pins.*

2 *Cut the blue pine into short lengths and pin them on to the garland.*

florist's wire
30cm/12in straw ring
carpet moss
German pins
blue pine
12 x 30cm/12in cinnamon sticks
6 large cones
3m/3¼yd x 7.5cm/3in wide ribbon
9 poppy seedheads
sisal string

3 *Wire the cinnamon sticks into three bundles and, using the German pins, attach them to the garland. Attach wires to the base of the cones by twisting them around the scales of the cones and pin them on to the garland close to the cinnamon sticks.*

Cut the ribbon into three pieces and fold each into a double bow using wire to secure the bows. Pin the bows to the garland over the cinnamon sticks and cones. Tuck the poppy seedheads into the folds of the bows and pin them in place. Tie three bows using the sisal string, fray the ends and then pin them on to the garland.

Right: *Soft blues and greens give this Christmas garland a Scandinavian look.*

MULLED WINE

In days past when folk rode on horses or took drafty carriages to their neighbours' houses at Christmas, mulled wine was a necessary restorative to the circulation. Today, most of us can travel in warmer and more comfortable conditions, but the taste and aroma of this spiced drink is an established part of Christmas.

Serves 10
2 bottles smooth red wine
½ tsp whole allspice berries
1 cinnamon stick
6 cloves
115g/4oz sugar
6 drops Angostura bitters
rind of ½ orange

Place all the ingredients in a saucepan and heat gently without boiling until the sugar has dissolved.

EGGNOG

This spectacular Christmas drink is for some unknown reason far more popular in America than in Britain.

Serves 6
6 large eggs, separated, at room temperature
200g/7oz caster sugar
300ml/½ pint/1¼ cups brandy
50ml/2fl oz/¼ cup dark rum
500ml/17fl oz/ 2¼ cups milk
120ml/4fl oz/½ cup double cream
15ml/1 tbsp vanilla essence
salt
freshly grated nutmeg

Using an electric mixer, beat the egg yolks until pale. Gradually mix in the sugar until the mixture thickens. Whisk in the brandy, rum, milk, cream and vanilla. In a separate bowl whisk the egg whites with a pinch of

Above: The heat of the mulled wine releases the fragrance of the cinnamon stick.

salt until they make soft peaks. Fold the whites into the yolk mixture and decant into a serving bowl. Chill for three hours. Before serving, stir the eggnog gently and sprinkle with freshly grated nutmeg.

BUTTERED RUM

A delicious alternative to mulled wine, this drink will warm the cockles of your heart.

Serves 6
4 cinnamon sticks
4 tsp soft brown sugar
120ml/4fl oz/½ cup dark rum
600ml/1 pint/2½ cups dry cider
25g/1oz unsalted butter
rind of ½ lemon
½ tsp ground mace

Warm four tisane glasses or mugs. Place a cinnamon stick, a teaspoon of sugar and a quarter of the rum in each glass. Gently heat the cider without boiling and pour it into the glasses. Top with butter, a curl of lemon rind and a sprinkling of mace.

GLÖGG

Glögg is an extremely potent and dramatically pyrotechnical drink which is great fun to serve at Christmas parties. It should be prepared and drunk with caution as you will discover from the instructions below.

Serves 6–8
4 whole allspice berries
muslin
4 cardamom pods
1 cinnamon stick
10 dried apricots, halved
2 bottles dry red wine
225g/8oz sugar cubes
600ml/1 pint/2½ cups aquavit or vodka, warmed
300ml/½ pint/1¼ cups cognac, warmed
nuts, unsalted
raisins

Tie the spices in a piece of muslin, place in a saucepan with the apricots and wine and heat. When the wine begins to simmer, remove the bag of spices and pour into a warmed heatproof bowl. Place a wire cake-rack over the bowl. Build a pyramid of the sugar cubes on the rack, making sure the construction is solid. Gently pour on the warmed aquavit or vodka and ignite at arm's length. Then pour on the cognac. Alternatively, ignite the aquavit or vodka in its pan and gently ladle it over the sugar. The sugar will melt as it burns and fall through the rack into the bowl. When the flames have died down, pour the drink into heatproof glasses or mugs, to which a few raisins and nuts have been added. Make sure that each person gets half an apricot.

Right: The rich colours of Christmas are enhanced by the glasses of mulled wine, which have been filled to welcome the guests.

FRESH DATE CAKE

Make this wonderful fat-free cake each year as a delicious, yet light alternative to the usual rich Christmas cake; the perfect antidote, to be eaten with a cup of lightly fragrant tea at the point when you never want to see another mince pie ever again.

Makes a 1kg/2¼lb cake
350g/12oz fresh dates
125g/4½oz glacé cherries
125g/4½oz self-raising flour
125g/4½oz caster sugar
½ tsp salt
225g/8oz coarsely chopped brazil nuts
25g/1oz shredded coconut, fresh if possible
1 large egg
30ml/2 tbsp brandy
Preheat the oven to 150°C/300°F/Gas 2.

Above: *Stuffed dates.*

Remove the skins from the dates, cut in half and remove the stones. Wash the cherries to remove the syrup and then quarter them. Sieve the flour, sugar and salt together into a large mixing bowl. Add the fruit, nuts and coconut and then toss so that every single ingredient is well coated with flour. Whisk the egg with the brandy, add it to the bowl and mix thoroughly.

Pour the mixture into a greased and lined 1kg/2¼lb loaf tin and bake for one and a quarter hours.

KUMQUATS AND LIMEQUATS IN BRANDY SYRUP

The yellow and green fruits are highly decorative as well as tasting very good indeed. Make a few extra jars to give to friends and family, and why not spoil yourself and open a jar for a treat and eat a few of the fruits spooned over vanilla ice cream.

Makes 500g/1lb 2oz, plus syrup
450g/1lb kumquats and limequats
175g/6oz sugar
150ml/¼ pint/⅔ cup brandy
1 tbsp orangeflower water

Using a toothpick, prick each individual fruit in several places. Dissolve the sugar in 300ml/½ pint/1¼ cups water over a gentle heat then bring to the boil. Add the fruit and simmer for approximately 25 minutes until it is tender. Drain the fruit and spoon into hot, sterilized jars. The syrup should be fairly thick; if not, boil for a few minutes, then allow to cool only very slightly. Add the brandy and the orangeflower water to the syrup. Pour the syrup over the fruit and seal immediately. Store in a cool place and use within six months.

Above: *Kumquats and limequats in brandy syrup.*

STUFFED DATES

Slivers of crystallized ginger give a bite to these fresh dates stuffed with marzipan and topped with halved walnuts. They are delicious served with coffee. Packed into a decorative box, they make an unusual gift.

24 fresh dates
50g/2oz crystallized ginger
115g/4oz marzipan
24 walnut halves

Using a sharp knife, slit the dates along their length and then carefully remove the stones. Chop the ginger into slivers and work them into the marzipan. Place a walnut-sized piece of marzipan in the cavity of each date and top with a halved walnut. The dates must be stored in the refrigerator and used within a week.

Right: *Home-made edible gifts are always much appreciated at Christmas.*

Seasonal Checklist

Evocative descriptions and timely reminders of tasks to be done throughout the year.

Spring

Spring is the season of new growth – of aromatic mint, broad-leaved sorrel and tender spikes of chives picked in their infancy to garnish young salad leaves or to pack in amongst baby vegetables freshly lifted from the garden and bottled for enjoying during the winter months. It is a time for flavoured butters drizzled over grilled vegetables and fish, of scented oils and vinegars and delicate flower cordials. It is the season of youth; all is green and yellow and there is a crisp, fresh fragrance in the air. It is a time of renewal when we spring clean our homes as unveiled windows reveal dusty corners, and we gently nourish our tender, winter-dried skin before we bare it to the warming sun.

IN THE GARDEN:
- Clean out the greenhouse and cold frame, washing down the windows and removing any dead or diseased plants.
- Sow flower, vegetable and herb seeds, making fortnightly sowings of salad crops.
- Cut early herbs for use in salads and flavoured oils and vinegars.
- Dig up early potatoes.

IN THE PANTRY:
- The pantry should be looking quite bare right now and this is a good opportunity to wipe down shelves and throw out anything that is past its best.
- Collect all the empty jars and bottles together, check that they have lids and replace rubber rings and seals where necessary.
- Bottle choice baby vegetables with new season herbs.
- Make flavoured oils, vinegars and mustards.

IN THE BATHROOM:
- Use the body scrub and washing grains to invigorate and cleanse the skin after winter.
- Make new batches of lotions, tonics and hair rinses.

IN THE STILL ROOM:
- Dry flower petals and herbs for future use in potpourris and scented sachets.
- Make a new batch of beeswax polish and furniture reviver ready for spring cleaning.
- Throw out any dried flowers and herbs that are looking tired and dusty and replace with fresh flowers picked from the garden.

SEASONAL CELEBRATION:
- Make a simnel cake at least two weeks before Easter Sunday.

Left: Bring a breath of spring into your home with daffodils, tulips and hyacinths, freshly cut from the garden.

Above: *An orchard is the perfect place to plant great banks of daffodils, but don't mow until they have died right down or every year they will produce fewer and fewer flowers.*

Right: *The delightful little crocus is one of the earliest and most cheerful of spring flowers, and even the least knowledgeable of windowsill gardeners should find space for a pot of these pretty flowers.*

Summer

As the sun climbs higher in the sky the greater heat it gives out intensifies taste and fragrance. The delicate flavours of spring give way to robust ripeness as tomatoes turn a deep luscious red and we marry their marvellous flavour with peppery basil and the fruitiest of olive oils. Strong flavours and colours are the order of the day: herbed mustards and marinades for barbecues; refreshing teas to be drunk in the shade; vibrant flowers and herbs, gathered in the morning when their fragrance is at its most intense for using fresh or for drying.

IN THE GARDEN:
- Move plants outside from the greenhouse and cold frame.
- Harvest herbs and flowers for drying.
- Dig up main crop potatoes and harvest onions, garlic and shallots.

IN THE PANTRY:
- Throw out the remnants of last year's dried herbs and replace with newly dried herbs.
- Bottle fruit and vegetables when they are in their prime.
- Make jams, jellies and curds from soft fruit.
- Blend herbal teas.

IN THE BATHROOM:
- Make herbal infusions and use in lotions, tonics and creams.
- Dry some herbs for use in later infusions.

Above: *The pleasure of being able to gather your own flowers from the garden is one of the joys of summer.*

IN THE STILL ROOM:
- Dry flowers for potpourris and arrangements.
- Make lavender bags and other scented sachets or dry the ingredients for use later.
- Make insect-repellent candles for use in the garden and near open windows.

SEASONAL CELEBRATION:
- Make sure you find time to sit and enjoy summer in the garden.

Left: *Sun-ripened tomatoes, freshly picked from the garden, have an intensity of colour and flavour that makes them irresistible.*

Left: *Summer yields a bounty of fresh garden salads which can be picked minutes before serving to enthusiastic diners at your al fresco dinner party .*

Below: *A warm wall in the garden is an ideal place for a fan-trained peach or apricot tree and can yield a surprisingly good harvest of fruit.*

151

A u t u m n

As the hedgerows stoop under the weight of ripening berries and the trees drop their leaves, the golden light of autumn burnishes all it touches. In woodlands, scurrying creatures gather food for the coming months and the air is rich with the scent of ripeness and decay. This is the time of year when the urge to preserve and store is at its strongest, when every country walk is an opportunity to gather, when even the most urbanized of us may make a pot of jam, taking pleasure in such a simple task. Children, however far removed from the land, pause to appreciate nature and the farmer at Harvest Festival or Thanksgiving.

Left: *Choose the variety of apple tree you grow with great care; it will be with you a long time and eating the fruit should be a pleasure not a chore.*

Below: *Autumn is the best time to go hunting for sweet chestnuts in local woods and meadows. Always check with an expert before eating.*

IN THE GARDEN:
• Pick fruit from the orchard and vegetables from the kitchen garden and store and preserve for winter.
• Bring tender plants into the greenhouse and cold frame.
• Pot up herbs for the kitchen windowsill.
• Gather seeds for drying ready to sow next year.

IN THE PANTRY:
• Make jams, jellies, pickles and chutneys.
• Prepare herb and spice mixes.
• Bottle fruit and vegetables.

IN THE BATHROOM:
• Make nourishing creams and lotions for face and body.
• Check through your essential oils and replace any that are too old or running low.
• Make up new batches of massage oils and lotions to revive tired muscles after clearing the garden.

IN THE STILL ROOM:
• Make beeswax candles.
• Make up dried flower arrangements and batches of potpourri

SEASONAL CELEBRATION:
• Make up a basket of produce for the Harvest Festival.
• Bake a harvest loaf.
• Make pumpkin lanterns and pumpkin pie for Halloween.

Right: *With their marvellous shapes and vibrant colours, squashes and gourds are wonderfully ornamental as well as full of flavour.*

Winter

Winter at its best is a bright crisp day with frost or snow underfoot, but all too often it is a procession of dreary grey days of unrelieved gloom, which can depress the most optimistic amongst us. This is the time of year when we can take pleasure in our earlier labours and feast on the flavours of spring and summer that are filling the shelves of our store cupboard. It is a time to nurture ourselves with delicious foods, to luxuriate in scented baths and to pamper ourselves with tempting sweetmeats. It is the season of giving, when we can make gifts for our friends and family and fill our homes with the smells of traditional spices that are an essential part of the Christmas festivities. It is a time to look forward, and in doing so, we complete the cycle and once again greet the coming of spring.

Above: *Those main crop vegetables that were stored in autumn now come into their own as they are used in warming soups and stews.*

Top: *Dried beans and pulses are a useful standby....*
Above: *... although still no match for fresh winter vegetables.*

IN THE GARDEN:
• Scrub pots and seed trays ready for seed sowing in the spring.
• Read the seed catalogues – and dream.
• Gather Christmas greenery early and stand in water in an outhouse or garage.

IN THE PANTRY:
• Enjoy using the fruits of your labours.
• Make sloe gin.
• Check the spice cupboard and replenish any stocks that are low.
• Use Seville oranges to make marmalade in January.
• Dry Seville orange skins for cooking and potpourris.
• Candy citrus peel.
• Make food presents ahead of the Christmas preparations.

IN THE BATHROOM:
• Make new batches of bath oils for winter dry skin.
• Prepare a new batch of hand cream and healing ointment.

IN THE STILL ROOM:
• Make bird treats to hang in the garden.

SEASONAL CELEBRATION:
• Make the Christmas garland at least two weeks before the festivities.

Above: *A well-stocked bird table will help many of the garden and woodland birds, not to mention the odd squirrel, survive through the harshest of winters, as well as providing you with hours of enchanting entertainment. Make sure you position it somewhere where cats cannot jump on to it.*

Right: *Between the vegetable garden and the cold frame you should be able to pick fresh vegetables and herbs all winter.*

Useful sources and suppliers

UK
Suppliers of essential oils

Neal's Yard Remedies
5 Golden Cross
Cornmarket Street
Oxford
OX1 3EU
Tel: 01865 245436 for mail order
catalogue.

Culpeper Ltd
Hadstock Road
Linton
Cambridge
CB1 6NJ
Tel: 01440 788196

Medicinal and culinary herbs

Potters Herbal Supplies
Leyland Mill Lane
Wigan
Lancs. WN1 2SB

Hambleden Herbs
Court Farm
Milverton
Somerset
TA4 1NF
Tel: 01823 401205

Natural beauty ingredients
G Baldwin & Co
173 Walworth Road
London SE17 1RW
Tel: 0171 703 5550

Dried flowers and potpourri
ingredients

The Hop Shop
Castle Farm
Shoreham
Sevenoaks
Kent
Tel: 01959 523919 for mail order service.

Robson Watley International (wholesale
quantities only)
2A Pembroke Road
Bromley
Kent BR1 2RU
Tel: 0181 466 0830

Mail order cut herbs and plants
Iden Croft Herbs
Tel: 01580 891432

US
Suppliers of essential oils

The Body Shop
45 Horse Hill Road
Cedar Knolls, NY 07927
Tel: (800) 541 2535

Kiehl's
109 Third Avenue
New York, NY 10002
Tel: (212) 677 3171

Lorann Oils
P O Box 22009
Lansing, MI 48909-2009
Tel: (800) 248 1302

Medicinal and culinary herbs

Cameron Park Botanicals
Highway 64 East
Raleigh, NC 27610

Caprilands Herb Farm
Silver Street
North Coventry, CT 06238

Seeds Blum
Idaho City State
Boise, ID 83706

Richter's Herb Catalog
Goodwood
Ontario
Canada
LOC 1AO

Dried flowers and potpourri ingredients

Dody Lyness Co.
7336 Berry Hill Drive
Polos Verdes Peninsula, CA 90274
Tel: (310) 377 7040

Gailann's Floral Catalog
821 W. Atlantic Street
Branson, MO 65616

Nature's Finest
P O Box 10311, Dept. CSS
Burke, VA 22009

Val's Naturals
P O Box 832
Kathleen, FL 33849
Tel: (813) 858 8991

AUSTRALIA
Suppliers of essential oils

Orton Australia
R.M.B. 4004A
Talgarno
Vic. 3691
Tel: (060) 201 136

Bridestowe Estate Pty Ltd
RSD 1597, Nabowla, Tas 7254
Tel: (003) 528 182

Medicinal and culinary herbs

Herbs of Gold Pty
Unit 5, 102 Bath Road
Krrawee, NSW 2232

Southern Light Herbs
P O BOx 227
Maldon, Vic. 3463

Dried flowers and potpourri ingredients

Yuulong Lavender Estate
Yendon Rd, Mt Egerton, Vic 3352
Tel: (053) 689 453

Hedgerow Flowers
177 King William Road
Hyde Park, SA 5061
Tel: (03) 9596 8742

Index

ACKNOWLEDGEMENTS

Thanks to:

Holly McIntntyre for her valued assistance with preparing projects and searching out props.

Liz Trigg for her help with the food projects.

Michelle for her inspired photography and good company.